CW00584992

MCDP 1-4

Competing

U.S. Marine Corps

PCN 142 000017 00

DEPARTMENT OF THE NAVY
Headquarters United States Marine Corps
Washington, D.C. 20350-3000

14 December 2020

FOREWORD

Western conceptions of the international struggle among nations (and other political actors) often use binary war or peace labels to describe it. The actual truth is more complicated. Actors on the world stage are always trying to create a relative advantage for themselves and for their group. Sometimes this maneuvering leads to violence, but the use of violence to achieve goals is more often the exception than the rule. Instead, most actors use other means in their competitive interactions to achieve their goals. The competition continuum encompasses all of these efforts, including the use of violence.

There are several reasons for explaining the competition continuum to Marines. The first is to make them aware that from "recruitment to retirement," they are an integral part of the Nation's strategic competition with other actors. *Marines are always competing, even when they are not fighting in combat.* Next, understanding unleashes creativity. Once Marines understand the nature and form of competition, their innovative spirit will lead to the development of new kinds of competitive advantages. Finally, this publication expands the discussion on how and where Marines fit into the continuum and where to look for their natural partners in competition.

By design, this is a small book with a construction that parallels Marine Corps Doctrinal Publication 1, *Warfighting*. It is not intended as a reference manual, but is designed to be read from cover to cover. This publication does not contain specific techniques or procedures we should adopt. Rather, it provides broad guidance in the form of concepts, with illustrations intended to stimulate thinking and encourage additional learning. It requires judgment in application.

We live in a time of renewed great power competition in an era of exponential technological and social change. Marines enjoy a rich heritage of advancing our Nation's interests in these kinds of struggles. As we look to the future, we must ensure today's—and tomorrow's—Marines do the same. Like maneuver warfare, competing is a way of thinking. We all need to read, study, and debate this publication with our fellow Marines. We must understand the importance of strategic competition and the essential role Marines play in it for our Nation.

DAVID H. BERGER
General, U.S. Marine Corps
Commandant of the Marine Corps

Publication Control Number: 142 000017 00

DISTRIBUTION STATEMENT A: Approved for public release; distribution is unlimited.

Competing

Chapter 1. The Nature of Competition

Competition Explained—The Continuum—War is a Special Kind of Competition—Competition Contains Many of the Same Attributes as War—*Ambiguity*—*Uncertainty*—*Boundary Stretching*—*Fluidity, Disorder, Complexity*—*The Human Dimension*—The Art, Science, and Dynamic of Competition—The Evolution of Competition—Conclusion

Chapter 2. The Theory of Competition

Competition as an Act of Policy—Competitive Advantage—Competitors as Systems—Means in Competition—*Attraction*—*Coercion*—*Information*—The Spectrum and Styles of Competition—The Threshold of Violence—Decision Making, Initiative, and Response—Conclusion

Chapter 3. Preparing for Competition

Competition and the Marine Corps—Campaigning Mindset—Professionalism—Education—Talent Management—Force Planning—Conclusion

Chapter 4. How Rivals Approach Competition

The Test—Differing Orientations—*Orientation's Effect on the OODA Loop*—*Language Shapes Behavior*—*Culture*—How Rivals View the Competitive Environment—Differing Approach to Competition Campaigning—A Rival Concept for Competition—*The Idea of "Theory of Victory" Applied to Competition*—*The Concept Illustrated*—Conclusion

Chapter 5. The Conduct of Competition

The Challenge—Maneuver Warfare's Influence—Orienting on the Competitor—Shaping the Action—Combined Arms—Campaign of Competition—Conclusion

Notes

Chapter 1

The Nature of Competition

Total war and perfect peace rarely exist in practice. Instead, they are extremes between which exist the relations among most political groups. This range includes routine economic competition, more or less permanent political or ideological tension, and occasional crises among groups.[1]

—MCDP 1, *Warfighting*

These words from the Marine Corps' warfighting philosophy frame the idea of competition for Marines. They also serve as a springboard for Marines to think about how they can contribute to winning the Nation's competitions, including the ones taking place below the threshold of violence.

Competition happens constantly in many forms amongst the nations of the world, in the diplomatic, informational, military, and economic arenas. Rivals often challenge each other in one of them while they cooperate in a different one. Competitors include a wide range of political actors, from nation-states to groups organized around a single cause. While the discussion below will often refer to state versus state rivalries, in most cases the ideas apply equally to challenges with non-state actors. Competition in various forms and among many different actors is the norm in international relations (understanding how others approach competition is critical, as discussed in chapter 4).

The Marine Corps participates in the competitions of the United States in many ways. Foremost among them is to fight and win our Nation's battles, and to be ready to do so at all times. (War itself is a special kind of competition. How it fits into the overall continuum will be explored in detail.) The very existence of the Marine Corps is a competitive act, as it signals to potential rivals that there are vital interests our Nation will go to war to protect, and that those of a maritime nature are important enough that we have invested in a dedicated naval expeditionary force to protect them. The capabilities the Marine Corps generates in preparation for battle are also competitive, as these capabilities are what help *deter* a potential rival from selecting a course of action above the threshold of violence.

The Marine Corps, however, does not "win" our Nation's competitions alone. In fact, the Marine Corps is most likely to *support* or *contribute to* advancing US interests as part of a larger competitive strategy. The Marine Corps can do a great deal to help the United States compete successfully, but it will do so as part of a larger national effort that extends well beyond the military instrument of national power.

From recruitment to retirement, Marines have the *potential* to help the Nation compete successfully in many ways. It starts with the right mindset, one that recognizes the Marine Corps' top priority is to win battles, while also recognizing that war and warfare are segments of a larger spectrum known as the *competition continuum*. Marines need to be clear-eyed about this spectrum. Even when Marines are not at war in one of its many forms, they are still in a state of competition. While demonstrating the ability to fight and win wars is crucial for deterrence, a successful US foreign policy will avoid wars (especially against great power rivals) whenever possible.

COMPETITION EXPLAINED

Competition is a fundamental aspect of international relations. As states and non-state actors seek to protect and advance their own interests, they continually compete for advantage.[2]

Nations and other political actors pursue their interests constantly and in a variety of ways. Competition results when the interests of one political group interact in some way with those of another group. These interactions take place in a dynamic environment. Each move an actor makes towards fulfilling an interest changes that ecosystem. Any interaction of interests changes the situation as well.

One approach for describing this environment uses the diplomatic, informational, military, and economic or DIME framework. These broad categories describe the kinds of tools political actors use in an effort to reach their goals. Often times tools from several categories are used together to fulfill interests or achieve goals. The gray box, *"Economic Competition: The Marshall Plan"* on the next page provides an illustration of an economic tool. It describes how financial aid to 17 countries in Europe after WW II was used by the United States to achieve post-war goals (diplomatic and informational tools supported this effort as well).[3]

Competitions are often labeled as "zero-sum" or "positive-sum." A zero-sum rivalry means that if one group achieves its goal then the rival group cannot achieve its own. A good example of zero-sum competition is when two nations struggle over the ownership of an island; in most cases only one of them can physically control it at a time. Positive-sum means that more than one group can make progress toward fulfilling interests or achieving goals at the same time. For example, two nations may compete economically, but both may see their gross domestic product (GDP) increase simultaneously.

Competition manifests itself in several ways, such as when one actor attempts to impose its will on others. Another way is when one competitor acts to frustrate another's plans, preventing them from achieving their goals. Both of those mainly apply to zero-sum struggles. In a positive-sum example, two economic rivals will try to best each other (like when they try to increase their market share in a particular industry at the expense of their rival) while both of their economies continue to grow.

Competition, especially at the nation-state level, is complex and it is *systemic*. For example, auto manufacturers in the United States compete with rival companies in the European Union and Japan, but this does not mean the US Government is also in direct competition with these governments, even though the auto manufacturers are based on their respective territories. Indirectly, the auto manufacturers may lobby their governments, asking them to take actions that favor their company in the global competition for auto sales. The individual actors are intertwined and interact with each other in many different ways. The details of this brief example are less important than it is for Marines to understand that strategic competition among international political actors is multi-layered and networked. Each competitor consists of many parts that interact in complex ways. As we see from these examples, competition and cooperation can coexist, and competition does not need to lead to conflict.

Economic Competition: The Marshall Plan

The European Recovery Program (better known as the "Marshall Plan") is a clear example of US economic competition following WW II. The stated goals of the plan were to rebuild war-torn areas of Europe, lower trade barriers, and modernize industry. In addition to improving prosperity and preventing the spread of Communism, the plan aimed to rehabilitate the economies of 17 countries to create the stable conditions needed for the survival of democratic institutions.

The plan was judged a success, providing $13B (over $128B in 2020 dollars) along with technical assistance. In addition to contributing to 15–25% growth in these countries during this period, it helped democracy grow despite the Communist threat.

THE CONTINUUM

There is no perfect model to use in explaining the competition continuum. The many feedback loops it contains make it very complex, so models will omit some details. However, models are useful because they help explain specific concepts and assist Marines in building their own visualization of the continuum.

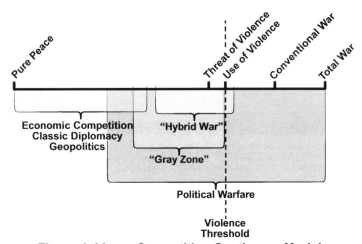

Figure 1. Linear Competition Continuum Model.

Figure 1 shows a linear model bounded by "pure peace" and "total war" (these boundaries are rarely, if ever, reached). This particular model shows different kinds of competitive acts in relation to the threshold of violence. It also clearly illustrates the wide spectrum of struggle that takes place between "peace" and "war," which helps us avoid the trap of thinking we are in a binary state of either "at peace" or "at war." *The actual condition is a more or less constant state of tension that in some cases crosses over the threshold of violence, only to recede again below the threshold.* Note that figure 1 is a model intended to help Marines think about the continuum. All Marines, and especially leaders, should study variations of this model. This will help develop a sense for how it could evolve over time or appear in different situations.

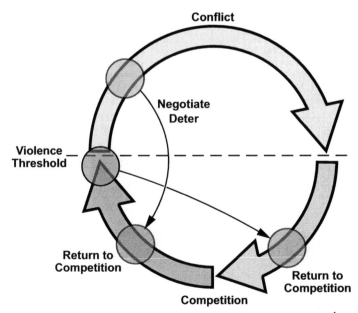

Figure 2. Circular Competition Continuum Model.[4]

In figure 2 we see a circular model that shows conflict above the violence threshold and competition below it. Starting at the bottom and moving around the circle in the direction of the main arrows, competition increases to a point just below the threshold. At this point, if the struggle does not cross into conflict, then one of many possibilities occurred. One of the actors could be *deterred* and the relationship returns to one of competition. The threat of violence could have been sufficient leverage and other rivals allowed the actor to achieve their goals, then the tension receded. Negotiations of some kind may have succeeded, bringing the actors back from the threshold. There are many possibilities on how rivals can turn away from the violence threshold and return to steady-state competition.

We also see that sometimes the threshold is crossed for a short time, only to jump back down into a state of competition below the violence threshold. Just as described above, note that deterrence is not the only thing that causes movement in this model. A competitor could move below the violence threshold again if it achieves its goals, or a negotiated bargain of some kind could cause similar movement. A thoughtful review of this model shows it has many uses.

However, make no mistake that the above models simply offer us different views to consider as we study strategic competition. All of the terms we use, including "conflict," "competition," "violence," and even "war" are part of an organic whole. All of these terms reside on a single continuum that describes the relationship between and among states in international relations. These political actors use activities at various points on the continuum to advance their interests and also set conditions to make it easier for them to achieve their interests in the future. This behavior is like a judo competition, when a competitor constantly tries to put the opponent off balance, sometimes through the application of violence, and sometimes by moving to a position of advantage. War itself is an integral part of this continuum, as we discuss below.

The gray box below describes some of the work of the State Department's George F. Kennan following World War II. Kennan was the author of the famous "Long Telegram" that described the

---

'The Inauguration of Organized Political Warfare'

Political warfare is the logical application of Clausewitz's doctrine in time of peace. In broadest definition, political warfare is the employment of all means at a nation's command, short of war, to achieve its national objectives.
—George Kennan (1948)

These opening words to Kennan's paper were directed to the National Security Council. The paper advocated for both overt and covert means to compete internationally, short of using violence.

In the Cold War struggle that was just beginning, Kennan stated the United States was handicapped by a belief that there is a "basic difference between peace and war . . . to view war as a sort of sporting contest outside of all political context." His work helped decision makers understand ideas like political warfare, which then helped the United States build the capabilities needed to successfully compete in the Cold War.

---

nature of the Soviet Union and alerted decision makers to the emerging Cold War and the need for the US Government to organize itself for political warfare.[5]

Kennan's diagnosis of the competition significantly shaped the way it unfolded across the whole of the US Government in the decades that followed. This highlights two important points for Marines. The first is the importance of accurately identifying the nature of the competition one faces. The way it is understood will affect the choices made in how to pursue the competition. An accurate appreciation will increase the chances for success. Second, Marines have an important but supporting role in strategic competition. This insight shapes the way we approach our competitive efforts.

WAR IS A SPECIAL KIND OF COMPETITION

Our warfighting philosophy informs us that *war* is a violent clash of interests between or among organized groups characterized by the use of military force. War is fundamentally an interactive social process. Its essence is a violent struggle between two hostile, independent, and irreconcilable wills, each trying to impose itself on the other. War's character can take many forms, from using military force to simply restore order during disaster relief operations to completely overturning the existing order within a society.[6]

War resides on the competition continuum above the threshold of violence. From a military perspective we also call the points along this scale above the threshold various forms of *armed conflict*. There are many descriptors of the forms that war takes, such as insurgency, hybrid, conventional, etc. *When we think of competition and war, the main points are to acknowledge that war is a political act that uses violence to achieve its aims, but it is also part of a spectrum of other competitive acts that do not use violence.*

In figure 2, the circular model of competition, conflict feeds back into competition. War sets the conditions for the character of the competition that follows it. War is like a violent move in a judo contest, its use can put a competitor into an advantageous position relative to an opponent. The gray box below discusses how the total military defeat of Japan in World War II set the

---

War Sets the Conditions for the Post-Conflict Competition

The defeat of Japan in WW II set the conditions for the post-war competition that followed. The United States imposed its will by drafting a new constitution that limited Japan to self-defense only.

This set the stage for the *cooperative* acts that followed, such as the US guarantee of Japan's defense from invasion by treaty. Somewhat like the Marshall Plan, the United States also provided economic aid to help restart the Japanese economy.

Japan rebuilt its economy in the 1950s and 60s, which led to it becoming a significant economic competitor for the United States, especially in the 1970s and 80s.

---

conditions for the competition that followed it. The US–Japan relationship is a good example of two nations who cooperate in many areas even as they compete in others. How the war was fought and its outcome significantly shaped that relationship and still affects it today.

COMPETITION CONTAINS MANY OF THE SAME ATTRIBUTES AS WAR

Ambiguity

Just like in war, ambiguity seems to be everywhere we turn in competition. As noted, two groups may try to best each other in one area while they cooperate in another, which can make the nature of the relationship between them unclear. The differences among rivals often clouds the picture as well. If the interests of two groups collide, but the interests of the first group are vital while those of the second group are a lower priority, there will be a mismatch between how the two groups view the competition. Sometimes the scale of the two rivals are so different it leads to ambiguity. For example, it took many years in the 1990s for the United States to conclude it was in a struggle with Al Qaeda, even as the competition bounced above and below the threshold of violence.[7]

Rivals often use or create ambiguity to cloak their actions. They do this to intentionally obscure their aims until it's too late for their competitors to react effectively. They want to use ambiguous acts to cause indecision, confusion, and hesitation.

Some actors appear ambiguous because they have internal divisions, multiple internal centers of power, or both. This includes national governments, reflecting the internal political competition taking place within them. These actors often do not speak with a single voice; from the outside their intentions can appear confusing or conflicting.

Uncertainty

Just as MCDP 1 states uncertainty is a pervasive trait of war, it is also a pervasive trait of competition. We make estimates of our competitor's designs and act accordingly. Uncertainty in international relations cannot be eliminated. It is nonlinear, meaning that a small amount of uncertainty can have a large effect on the situation. Dealing with it means one is also dealing with *risk*.

Often a competitor's goal is to use ambiguity to inject uncertainty into a situation so their rival will hesitate to act, using it to take incremental steps toward their ultimate goal. This approach is known as *gradualism* or *salami-slicing*; each step taken is by itself so small it does not cause a significant reaction from an opposing group. Eventually, the sum of the small steps will result in reaching the goal. Actors also make use of ambiguity and uncertainty to cause enough hesitation so they can reach their goal while their competitor tries to make sense of the situation. By the time the competitor figures it out, the goal is achieved, which is called a *fait accompli* (something already done).

Boundary Stretching

Boundary (or threshold) stretching occurs when an actor uses measures short of war to force movement or change in the nature of a boundary to gain greater regional influence, access, and control.[8] By "boundary," we mean a limit of some kind that if crossed would normally trigger a significant reaction. Before the boundary stretching events occur, most people would assume crossing a redline would cause a violent response of some kind. The goal of the actor using boundary stretching is to achieve their goals in such a way that a response is not triggered (or if a response happens, it does not result in a state of war between the actors). When this happens, we often see a new limit established; the boundary has been "stretched" (see the gray box on the next page, "*Russia Exploits and Stretches Thresholds in Eastern Europe*").[9]

Fluidity, Disorder, Complexity

While interests usually remain stable for long periods of time, the ways and means groups use to reach them change constantly. The efforts by groups to try different approaches produces fluidity, while each action changes the environment as well. Actors see the new structure and adapt to it, changes that often increase the level of disorder. International competition is disorderly, as multiple actors strive to reach their goals using all the tools at their disposal. These observations are consistent with systems theory. We change the system whenever we interact with it, often in unpredictable ways.

Russia Exploits and Stretches Thresholds in Eastern Europe

Russia devised ways to stretch the threshold for when the international community would decide to counter their actions against nations that were part of the former Soviet Union. It did this when they intervened in Georgia and South Ossetia in 2008. Even though Georgia had a West-leaning leader and contributed troops to the coalitions in Iraq and Afghanistan, Georgia was not part of NATO or the European Union. There was little legal justification for US counterintervention in Georgia, while the United States was also pre-occupied with the wars in Iraq and Afghanistan. Thus there was no clear threshold (or boundary) for when the United States or NATO would counter a Russian incursion into a former Soviet nation.

While it's not clear if Russia had Georgia in mind when it seized part of Ukraine in 2014, the overall approach paralleled the strategy used against Georgia. The tactics it used were sophisticated and deliberately calibrated to avoid crossing US or NATO thresholds for a military response.

With a combination of graduated covert and overt tactics, the Russian military was able to create just enough doubt and confusion to delay a response; in short order the presence of Russian special forces on Ukrainian soil was normalized. These military elements were also matched with sophisticated Russian diplomatic and informational activities, such as a rapid parliamentary vote to annex Crimea and aggressive use of offensive cyber and the media.

While not completely without costs (especially sanctions), Russia took advantage of a boundary originally stretched in Georgia to achieve their goals in Ukraine.

The above factors and their constant change create a great deal of complexity in the environment. This complexity is also systemic and therefore nonlinear, as small changes in one aspect of competition can cause big impacts in other areas. Because change is a constant and actors continually adapt to changes in an effort to achieve competitive advantages, complexity runs throughout the competition continuum. Marines must learn to thrive in this environment, instead of trying to create order in the vain hope of avoiding complexity.

The Human Dimension

As the Nation's force-in-readiness, Marines will often find themselves involved in competitions that are close to the threshold of violence. The *threat of violence* acts on the human brain in much the same way as experiencing actual violence acts on it. The two are not synonymous, because actually experiencing violence is clearly more coercive than the threat of it. Yet, we must be aware of how the threat of violence affects human decision making, because even its threat can cause a physical and emotional response in people. This increases the potential for misjudgment, over reaction, and other mistakes. It also could be a source of competitive advantage for those who can control their emotions in the heat of the moment so that they can make sound decisions.

A nation's culture and its effect on how people think also affects the choices they make. For example, some cultures promote holistic thinking while others value a more analytical thought process. Some value action, which can create an implicit bias toward regularly choosing the most aggressive course of action.

The list of potential cultural influences is a long one. Thus, culture will have an impact on many aspects of competition, including decision making and how information is perceived. Understanding the human dimension of competition is an area needing constant study by Marines.

THE ART, SCIENCE, AND DYNAMIC OF COMPETITION

The Marine Corps, as part the joint force, plays an essential role in securing national aims in conditions sometimes regarded as outside of the military sphere: competition below the threshold of armed conflict and the often lengthy consolidation of gains that inevitably follows war.[10] To play this role successfully, Marines need the ability to see and understand the competitive forces in the environment, understand what tools are available to them, and be able to envision how they can contribute to a campaign of competition.

Creativity or art is necessary to imagine different ways and means for Marines to contribute to reaching these aims. Constructing a set of steps along a timeline to help reach them, along with the necessary feedback loops to improve performance over time, are abilities that align with the science of competition. In many ways this is nothing new. It comes down to sizing up your opponent with a critical eye and then coming up with a creative solution that allows you to achieve your goals, despite the opponent's resistance. Marines have done this for ages.

The nature of these campaigns will require Marines to get comfortable asking for authorities to use tools in new domains (like cyber or support to public diplomacy). These campaigns combine cooperation and competition with the other DIME instruments of power (including armed conflict, if necessary) to achieve and sustain strategic objectives. In most cases avenues already exist to request these authorities, usually through the chain of command up to the relevant combatant commander. This is part of the mindset shift, because Marines will need to determine how they can support a comprehensive strategy, in which they will often need to identify and make use of joint and interagency capabilities if they are to fully participate in a competition campaign. Again, this is not new. There are many examples of Marine expeditionary units and special purpose MAGTFs having done the planning and staff work needed to operate effectively with these joint and interagency tools.

THE EVOLUTION OF COMPETITION

International competition is never static; it constantly evolves. In fact it is co-evolutionary, because as one actor develops a competitive tool, other actors adapt to it by trying to either counter it or develop another tool that displaces it. This co-evolution is seen clearly when technology changes. Henry Ford's

---

The Co-evolution of Concepts

Before, during, and after WW II, the joint force worked to perfect the concept of power projection, which broadly speaking is the ability to deliver enough combat power to win in battle anywhere on the globe. For example, the aircraft carrier strike group is a major component of the power projection concept.

Since WW II, other nations observed how the US power projection concept worked. In recent decades, some nations took advantage of rapid technological change and developed the anti-access/area denial or A2AD concept. Part of this concept is specifically designed to prevent carrier strike groups from getting close enough to their shores to project power.

Now, the co-evolution continues as the joint force searches for ways to overcome A2AD.

invention of the assembly line caused dramatic efforts to adapt among other auto makers. In today's world, firms increasingly try to automate their assembly lines in an effort to stay ahead in the competitive marketplace.

In much the same way, the choices political actors make in developing new concepts and the technology to support them are competitive acts. They develop them because they seek an advantage over a particular rival or rivals. The speed of this evolution usually rests on the rate of technological change, because new technologies create opportunities to develop new concepts (or new concepts may stimulate the development of new technology). In some cases though, new concepts emerge when mature technologies are combined with new organizations and new operating methods. As militaries wrestle with the questions of how to build and keep an edge over their potential opponents, they juggle factors like *switching costs* (How much money and effort does it take to make a change?); the *cost curve* (Will I spend more or less than my opponent? How long can I sustain the level of spending this change requires?); and *opportunity cost* (If I put effort into this change, then I will not be able to do something else instead.).

Marines know that in combat, sometimes we fight to gain information about the enemy. Once we obtain this information, we then inject it into our plans so that we increase the effectiveness of our operations. The same dynamic exists in competition. We gain information as we compete with a rival and must use this to our advantage. MCDP 1 teaches that we should try to "get inside" the enemy's thought processes and see the enemy as they see themselves. This holds equally for "getting inside" our competitor's thoughts processes, which we will explore further in chapter 4.

CONCLUSION

Competition is the normal state of the relationship between political actors in international relations. It occurs as the interests of these actors come into conflict as they try to advance them in the world. Oftentimes two political actors will compete in one area and cooperate in another; thus there is a competition continuum that extends from relatively benign efforts to advance interests to the violent efforts that include war. War, then, is a special kind of competition, one that sets the conditions for the (mostly) non-violent struggle that always follows the end of armed conflict.

Like war, competition is characterized by ambiguity, uncertainty, fluidity, disorder, and complexity. Rivals will try to use these attributes to obscure their aims and achieve advantages over their opponents. Competitors naturally apply creativity and science to develop advantages as well, which causes the form of competition to constantly evolve. The history of competition is also the history of change.

Marines and the Marine Corps have an important but supporting role in the Nation's competitions. The activities of Marines take place all along the continuum, including on both sides of the violence threshold. The competition continuum is therefore something that Marines must understand.

Chapter 2

The Theory of Competition

COMPETITION AS AN ACT OF POLICY

As states engage in competition, or try to shape the competitions ongoing among the range of state and non-state actors involved in areas of interest to states, they develop policies to frame, order, and apply resources to this activity. Marines need to understand policy, how it is developed, and how it relates to ongoing competition. Marines are frequently asked to provide input to policy makers as they deliberate. Understanding the larger context around policy decisions helps Marines determine the broader intent behind specific decisions, which in turn helps us make sound supporting plans.

Like war, Marines should think of competition as serving policy. Since we acknowledge competition as an enduring condition in international relations, then we need to take an equally long view when it comes to policy as well. Vital US interests have remained relatively stable over time. For example, since WW II they have been framed in various ways while consistently calling for maintenance of our Constitutional values, protection of the American homeland and people, promotion of American prosperity, and advancement of American influence in the world.[11] The contemporary environment will affect the specifics of policy, but the enduring foundation for it consists of stable interests such as these.

Enduring interests provide Marines a potential source of *competitive advantage*. Adhering to our values, when done as part of a comprehensive strategy, can serve to attract others and work in harmony with what Marines learned from an early age. Values such as freedom of expression and press freedom can help frustrate the plans of some competitors. Positive-sum interests, such as increasing American prosperity, also help

---

**Freedom of Navigation:
An Enduring US Interest**

Since the founding of the Nation, the United States has asserted a vital national interest in preserving freedom of the seas. One of the first missions of the US Navy was to defend US commercial vessels in the Atlantic Ocean and Mediterranean Sea from pirates and other maritime threats. In 1918, President Woodrow Wilson made "freedom of the seas" point number two in his Fourteen Points speech to Congress. In 1979, the United States initiated a Freedom of Navigation Program to contest "unilateral acts of other states designed to restrict the rights and freedom of the international community."

Since 1979, every US President has directed the State Department and Department of Defense to implement the FoN Program.

---

attract allies and partners. This is especially true when we can show how their interests align with ours.

Domestic politics affects the policy decisions of almost all competitors and the resulting character of nearly all competitions. As mentioned in chapter 1, there are often multiple centers of power in each nation and the struggle amongst them often creates ambiguity in the minds of outside observers. These struggles affect internal politics and often drive—or limit—current policy choices. This is true in the United States; for example, when we see the deliberations on national policy among the three co-equal branches of government. In other, less open societies, domestic considerations have major impact on policy even though these considerations are often harder for outsiders to understand.

For United States Marines, understanding current policy relies in part on understanding the interplay between domestic politics and our enduring vital national interests. Aspects of domestic politics, like the election cycle and contemporary societal issues, affect current policy. These aspects are typically felt by Marines through such things as resourcing decisions, guidance on the composition of the force, and specific direction to focus on particular national interests or particular competitors.

International competition, particularly among nations, plays out over a long timeline. Pursuing the goals put forth by the Constitution and its amendments has been an enduring vital interest of the United States since the day it became effective in 1789. This contrasts with our desire to bring war to a conclusion as quickly as possible. Marines need to understand this distinction.

COMPETITIVE ADVANTAGE

"Advantage" is relative to a competitor, when one actor is able to do something better than its rival or rivals. A business enjoys a competitive advantage when it can sell a product at a lower price than other businesses, assuming other factors, like quality, stay the same. Nations also have relative competitive advantages (also referred to as comparative advantages). Historically, the innovative culture in the United States helped it bring new goods and services to the international marketplace faster than others. The cost of labor in some countries is lower than in others, which makes them more attractive for labor-intensive manufacturing businesses. It follows then that we must understand our potential rivals if we are to develop and maintain a competitive advantage over them.

The United States has many competitive advantages in international competition. The world's largest economy and an international financial system that uses the dollar to make transactions are strong economic advantages. The enduring US interest in freedom of navigation on the seas attracts many partners, because free navigation reduces the overall cost of trading between nations. The US higher education system attracts students from all over the world. The list can go on, but these illustrations show that we should look for a nation's competitive advantages among its enduring qualities in areas such as its values, interests, and culture.

The competitive advantages in the military component of DIME are naturally of great interest to Marines. Since WW II, the United States made use of several military advantages such as the joint force's ability to project and sustain power globally, its skill at operating across domains, and its expertise in precision targeting and strike. The US military's principled professionalism can also present distinct advantages, for example when it is properly contrasted with competitors seeking to extend authoritarian government, without regard for the rule of law or protection of civilians.

Note that these competitive advantages exist across the competition continuum and not only in time of war. We conduct exercises in part to demonstrate that the United States has a military capability it could use if necessary. The existence of these capabilities can *impose cost* on a potential rival, because the rival may need to expend resources if they want to overcome or negate a US competitive advantage as the rival pursues their goals.

**Operation Outside the Box
Demonstrates a Competitive Advantage**

Operation Outside the Box on 6 September 2007 was an Israeli airstrike on a suspected Syrian nuclear reactor. The strike was judged successful but it was not publicized at the time; Israel did not acknowledge the attack until 2018. However, most observers attributed the attack to Israel.

Notably, the Israeli air force used cyberwarfare tools to defeat the extensive Syrian air defense system. Israel was able to achieve its aims despite these significant defenses, and their ability to do so demonstrated one of their competitive advantages. According to one analysis, the "raid on Syria was a strategic signal . . . about deterrence more than creating damage."

When viewed from this perspective, we gain insight into how a military competitive advantage can help us compete with a rival.[12]

Also note that it needs to be a conscious decision on when and how to reveal our most sensitive competitive advantages. At minimum, we should leverage such revelations for advantage in the information element of power. Other capabilities might be cloaked in secrecy until they actually need to be used.

All types of competitive advantages can atrophy, however. They need appropriate practice, exercising, and improving if they are to remain advantages in the dynamic environment of international competition.

COMPETITORS AS SYSTEMS

Competitors are *complex adaptive systems*, meaning they have many parts and these parts interact with each other in nonlinear, often unpredictable, ways. Consider Iran's national security decision-making structure. To some outside observers, it may appear to function as a strictly hierarchical organization with all important decisions being made by the supreme leader and president at the top of the pyramid. However, the real story is more complex. Much of the supreme leader's authority comes from the informal relationships he has with top commanders in the national security infrastructure and through the presence of his clerical representatives in military organizations. Even though the president is the chairman of the Supreme Council for National Security, his power ebbs and flows because the supreme leader is the commander in chief and may bypass the president through his informal relationships. The military structure itself can act in unpredictable ways, especially the Islamic Revolutionary Guards Corps (IRGC). The IRGC has developed significant (and separate) political power based on its financial resources, because it controls many businesses in almost every sector of the Iranian economy.[13] Each of these power centers (among others) jockeys for power inside Iran, working to advance their own internal or domestic interests. Thus in a fictional example, an Iranian national security decision to act more aggressively against oil tankers in the Arabian Gulf likely emerged from a complex interaction. The IRGC might have sponsored the action because they want to try and drive up oil prices for internal economic reasons. The supreme leader might want to increase his influence by allowing this action and therefore empowering IRGC commanders he favors. And the president might go along with this decision because he wants the supreme leader's support in a different area not related to national security. This brief illustration shows just a few of the many possible interactions that sum up into sometimes unanticipated results. Consideration of how factors like these can interact starts to give us some insight into the systemic nature of such competitors.

Developing a model of how a competitor's system fits together helps identify their competitive strengths and weaknesses. At a basic level, each of these systems consist of people, ideas, and things. The people make the system work. They also analyze its performance over time, because they are also responsible for sustaining or improving the system's competitive advantages. The ideas of the system are found in the goals it pursues and in the concepts and processes it uses to operate in the world. (Mao famously stated, "Politics is war without bloodshed while war is politics with bloodshed." This quote suggests a mindset that blurs the lines between peace and war; the mindset this idea creates may give a competitor an advantage in operating near the threshold of violence. We will develop this further in chapter 4.)

Ideally, things are then added or created to support the people and ideas within the system, helping it to achieve its goals. With this in mind, we can look at a competitor's system to create a model of how it fits together, where it is strong, and where it is vulnerable. Finally, after creating this model Marines must remain disciplined in its use. Models are useful but imperfect; they are our theories about the systemic structure of our rival. We need to remain alert for opportunities to improve our models as we learn more about how our competitors actually operate in the real world.

We also look at our own system to increase our competitive advantages or to create new ones. For example, do the people in our system have the necessary skills and aptitudes required to sustain our competitive advantages? Do they have the skills to build new ones? At a national level, does the target population for our recruiting efforts have the right education? In a similar way, we can look at our ideas (Do our operating concepts give us advantage?) and things (Does any of our equipment provide overmatch?) to evaluate the competitiveness of our system. Oftentimes it is the combination of these elements that provides a competitive advantage. It is not always true that the organization with the newest or most equipment wins the competition. Sometimes the side that is able to combine adequate material with innovate ideas becomes the winner. From this analysis, we can then increase our existing advantages or create new ones as deemed necessary.

MEANS IN COMPETITION

As similarly described in *Warfighting*, the highest level of competition involves the use of all the elements of power. Marines are primarily concerned with the military aspects of competition, but we must not consider it in isolation from the other elements of national power. MCDP 1 states the "use of military force may take any number of forms from the mere deployment of forces as a demonstration of resolve to the enforcement of a negotiated truce to general warfare with sophisticated weaponry." Here we see the alignment between our warfighting and competition doctrines start to emerge.

In war we impose our will on our adversary, their cooperation is not required. In competition, we make use of military force to *attract* or *coerce*. When using attraction, we use incentives to induce a rival (or other political actor) to adopt a position favorable to us or to otherwise allow us to reach our goals.

When using coercion, we compel a rival to take an action in our favor (or to stop taking an action that is not in our favor), or we make use of military force to deter a rival from taking action in the first place. For both compellence and deterrence, our goal is to use the *threat of military force* to achieve our desired outcome. For this to be the case, our competitive advantage must be clear enough to our rival that it affects the decisions they make. Note that competitive advantage does not necessarily equal military superiority. A competitor's strength of will, along with the nonmilitary tools of policy, are part of the equation, too.

Attraction

Political actors often use various forms of *attraction* to achieve their goals. To attract someone is to induce, entice, or persuade someone into doing something. In a negotiation, it is a reward or incentive for someone to make a choice that is favorable to us. We can say then that attraction is the counterpoint to coercion: instead of using pressure to help us reach our goals, we use some type of reward instead.

Marines participate in attraction strategies all the time, such as when demonstrating our professional commitment to our national values or when conducting bi-lateral training. In recent years for example, as part of a larger US attraction strategy Marines provided training on amphibious operations to an important ally, Japan.

There are many familiar instances of the United States using competitive attraction strategies across all elements of national power, such as collective security treaties like NATO, the Fulbright Scholars Program, and most-favored nation trading status. The gray box below on *"The Huk Rebellion"* illustrates a case when the United States used many elements of national power (including military) to help an ally, the Philippines. In turn, this multi-layered aid attracted and sustained the Philippines as an ally in the United States' global competition with communism.

**The Huk Rebellion:
The Military Contribution to a Strategy of Attraction**

In 1950, the Philippine government was pushed to the verge of collapse by a well organized, popularly supported, communist insurgency known as the Hukbalahap. No stranger to internal rebellion, the nation again faced a direct challenge to democratic government. The United States, already at war in Korea, was threatened with the loss of a strategic stronghold in the Pacific, and the subversion of a longtime friend and ally.

Those opening words from *The Hukbalahap Insurrection* provide the context for the story about how the United States employed a comprehensive attraction strategy to achieve its goals in the competition against communism in the mid-20th century. The United States used diplomatic tools and significant economic aid to support the Philippines in their effort to defeat the insurrection. In addition, the United States provided a military assistance group that played an important role, especially in the close working relationship then-LtCol Edward Lansdale built with Ramon Magsaysay (first as defense secretary and then as president).

This remarkable story provides an illustration of how the United States used all elements of national power in a successful competitive strategy of attraction.

Coercion

Political actors often use *coercion* as a way to achieve their goals. To coerce someone is to pressure, intimidate, or force someone into doing something, or to reach one's goals through the use of pressure, threat, or force. It does this by influencing an adversary's will or incentive structure. It is a strategy that often combines the threat of force, and if necessary the limited and controlled use of force, with positive inducements. Coercion has two forms, *compellence* and *deterrence*. Compellence is a threat intended to make an adversary *do* something, to take a specific action (or to stop taking it once it has already started). Deterrence is a threat intended to *inhibit* an adversary from taking a particular action, to prevent it from even getting started. In both cases, the target of the coercion must cooperate, because the target must decide to comply with the goal of the actor who is applying the coercion. This cooperation is not friendly or willing, but it still must exist for coercion to be effective.[14, 15, 16] The gray box on the next page describes a case when the United States used compellence to induce other nations to take particular actions.

For familiar examples of deterrence, think of the many times in decades past that the National Command Authorities decided to put a MEU off the coast of a nation in order to discourage leaders from taking a particular action. For this approach to succeed, the decision makers in that nation needed to accept that the threat presented by the MEU was significant enough for them to decide to comply with the US position. Deterrence occurred only when the target nation's decision makers decided that the threat represented by the MEU outweighed the benefit they would receive from taking the action they originally intended.

> **The Suez Crisis and Coercion**
>
> In July 1956, the leader of Egypt Gamal Abdel Nasser announced the nationalization of the Suez Canal. In response, Britain, France, and Israel came up with a plan to seize the canal. The conspirators did not consult with the administration of President Eisenhower, assuming he would support them once the operation began.
>
> For several reasons, Eisenhower determined the United States could not support the allies in their operation. The most important reason was the vital US national interest of keeping the Soviet Union out of the Middle East.
>
> The Eisenhower administration first tried communicating the lack of US support and strong desire for the operation to cease to Britain, France, and Israel. When this did not cause them to stop, Eisenhower threatened to sell British bonds held by the US Government, which would have heavily damaged the fragile post-war British economy. This coercive use of the economic element of national power caused the operation to end, with the invaders being replaced by UN peacekeepers.

The idea of using coercion in a competition can be misleading if we do not identify the assumptions that support its use. It is often assumed that a stronger nation can naturally coerce a weaker one into doing what it wants. However, this assumption may not be true if the weaker nation is willing to absorb more punishment than the stronger one can or will deliver, or stay committed to its goals over a longer period. We call this *asymmetry of interests* (in this case, the weaker nation has a more powerful desire to achieve its interests than that of the stronger nation). The gray box on the "*Cod Wars*" provides an example of this asymmetry.

"The Cod Wars" and Asymmetry of Interests

Four times between 1952 and 1976, the United Kingdom and Iceland entered into disputes about fishing rights in Icelandic waters. These disputes were between NATO allies who also shared economic interests; they sharply competed in some areas while cooperating in others.

Iceland expanded its zone of exclusive fishing rights in each successive dispute. The UK resisted these moves, citing historic claims to these fishing grounds. The UK government also wanted to support the economies of the fishing villages that relied on the catch from waters near Iceland. However, Iceland's interests were stronger. They viewed the disputes as attacking their national sovereignty and fishing was a much greater portion of their national economy.

Both nations committed significant military, informational, diplomatic, and economic resources to the competition. The UK employed the Royal Navy to protect British fishing trawlers while in some instances Iceland's patrol boats used net cutters against British fishing boats. Britain threatened economic sanctions at various times while Iceland threatened to withdraw from NATO and close a US base on the island.

Ultimately, Iceland's domestic politics and vital national interests caused them to have greater commitment to achieving their aims, which led to them succeeding, despite the UK having much greater economic and military power.

Information

Information plays a special role in competition. *Narratives* play an important part because they are what gives meaning to a set of facts. For example, two competitors may both desire to possess a particular island. One of them may have a narrative that explains their claim to the island on the basis of its historical ownership of it. The other may have a narrative that says some of their people currently use the island, and current possession makes their claim stronger. The two narratives compete with each other to give the fact its meaning. To defeat a narrative, it must be replaced by another one. Simply trying to negate someone else's narrative is not sufficient.

Information works similarly for military force in general and Marines in particular. A narrative exists about the deterrent quality of the United States Marine Corps. Marines have a reputational advantage based on a history of success in battle, adherence to high standards, and adaptability. The Marine Corps' ability to adapt, whether for amphibious warfare, vertical envelopment, or the next emerging challenge is a critical part of this narrative as well. The very existence of a relevant and capable Marine Corps can be seen as a cost-imposing measure on our competitors.

Demonstrating a capability at an exercise and then communicating so that it affects a competitor's thinking is another way Marines use information. Leaders determine what capabilities to reveal and when to reveal them as part of a larger approach. However much is specifically revealed, publicizing adherence to high standards in realistic training can help sustain the Marine Corps' reputational advantage and affect the thinking of our Nation's competitors.

Marines need to understand the impact of culture when they use information as a competitive tool. Cultural differences affect how narratives are interpreted by various audiences. One message might be understood in one country in a way that is significantly different from how it is understood in another. Marines must account for this and focus the narratives we use so that our target audience understands our message in the way that we intend.

THE SPECTRUM AND STYLES OF COMPETITION

The usual condition of international relations is one of competition across the elements of national power. When we consider the spectrum of choices and the different styles to choose from on the competition continuum, we should look again at a diagram like figure 2, on page 1-7.

Below the violence threshold we typically see activities from the non-military aspects of national power. For example, economic competition is seen at the national level in the struggle for market share in a particular industry or in the effort to negotiate favorable terms in a trade agreement. Moving clockwise on the spectrum we might see sharper economic acts like industrial espionage, the theft of intellectual property, or the use of sanctions.

As we move clockwise to the lower left quadrant of figure 2, we would expect to see competitors employing activities that are often labeled as hybrid warfare, gray zone warfare, or political warfare; many additional labels have been used to identify similar sets of activities. In each of these forms, competitors may use the threat of violence and individual violent acts to affect the decision making of their opponents. Competitors also use ambiguity and uncertainty to cause rivals to hesitate. This can include overt, covert, and illegal activities, irregular tactics, terrorism, criminal behavior, etc., all working together to help achieve desired political objectives.[17, 18] Both sides consciously strive to stretch boundaries in an effort to increase their freedom of action, effectively moving the threshold line in figure 2 "up" in the diagram. Repetitive actions can also move the line up or down over time. The gray box on *"Gradualism and Salami-Slicing"* on the next page illustrates these kinds of repetitive, numbing cycles. Competitors use these activities in an effort to achieve their aims without provoking a state of war, or even a strong reaction from a particular nation or the international community in general.

The above is not an exhaustive list. For millennia, human creativity has produced many styles of competition at various points on the continuum. These styles often incorporate the violence threshold and the affect it has on human decision making. Political actors then posture in ways that take advantage of the threat of violence, or brief violent acts, to achieve their aims. The only limit seems to be the extent of human imagination.

In addition to competing through attraction, coercion, and the various forms illustrated above, Marines can also compete by *imposing costs*. We impose costs on a rival when we develop a credible capability and a rival must spend resources in order to try

Gradualism and Salami-Slicing

The People's Republic of China makes an *ambiguous* claim to the South China Sea, represented by a "nine-dashed line" inherited from a 1946 Republic of China map. The line encompasses nearly the entire sea and all its hundreds of small features, putting China into maritime and territorial disputes with most neighbors.

Through a series of persistent actions since the 1950s, China has demonstrated determination to coerce neighbors into abandoning their claims to own the features and ceding their lawful resource rights.

With gradual, *salami-slicing* tactics, Chinese forces have taken competitive steps that accumulate into *de facto* Chinese control of much within the "nine-dashed line." Even though others largely do not recognize or accept China's steady encroachment, no individual step has crossed the threshold and triggered an organized military or diplomatic response.

Many of these competitive acts, including frequent use of ramming and water cannons against foreign fishing and law enforcement vessels, are near/below the violence threshold. In 2012, China used coast guard and maritime militia forces to evict the Philippines from Scarborough Reef without firing a shot. China has also established a considerable military presence on key features (even creating some from dredged reefs to build large fortifications). It has strengthened coast guard and militia forces that make credible threats of violence against other claimants, deterring them from exercising their rights and using maritime space.

and counter it. For example, the Department of Defense has experienced increasing cyber attacks in the past decades. This has imposed costs, because the Department of Defense has to spend time and money to develop training for every service member and civilian to counter these attacks (among other actions). The time people then spend conducting training is an opportunity cost, because they are not using that time to do something else. Note that we can impose costs on a competitor at any point along the competition continuum. While we normally think of doing so below the threshold of violence, we can also impose costs during war when we force an adversary to divert resources from their preferred actions in order to counter one of our capabilities.

THE THRESHOLD OF VIOLENCE

The threat of violence and violent acts are competitive tools in international relations. The goal of posturing is to affect the decision making of the target, to make them so fearful of the damage they might receive if the posturing escalates to violence that they submit and let the posturer achieve their goals (and it places one into a favorable position, should violence follow). In some cases, the posturing briefly crosses the threshold and violence occurs to demonstrate the resolve of the actor. This brief use of violence still has the same aim, which is to affect the target's decisions.

Many actors intentionally try to obscure or confuse exactly where this threshold lies. They do this to cause enough ambiguity and hesitation that they can achieve their aims with little or no interference. This has been true historically and it will likely increase in the future. Some rivals use capabilities, like certain cyber and space activities, that have destructive effects but fall short of some definitions of violence in an effort to obscure whether or not they have crossed the threshold.

In support of US goals, Marines perform missions on both sides of the violence threshold seen in figure 1, on page 1-6. On the right side of the spectrum, the Marine Corps has a rich history of contributing to the Nation during conventional war (World Wars I and II are clear examples). The Marine Corps has an equally rich history on the left side of the spectrum. There are many examples of the National Command Authorities positioning a MEU off the coast of a competing nation in order to compel them to take an action, or putting Marines ashore to deter a political group from attacking an embassy. There are also many examples of a MEU performing disaster relief operations and contributing to attraction, by communicating through the informational element of national power that the United States is an altruistic actor.

In some cases, Marines were introduced into a situation below the violence threshold, but then a political group performed a violent act against US interests. The disciplined response of the Marines then occurred above the violence threshold, but the violence was limited and it did not reach the level of conventional war. Following these brief periods of violence the competition again fell below the violence threshold (in most cases).

DECISION MAKING, INITIATIVE, AND RESPONSE

Marines are taught that decision making is essential since all actions are the result of decisions or of non-decisions. If we lack the will required to make a decision, then we have willingly surrendered the initiative to our foe. If we consciously postpone taking action for some reason, that is also a decision.

Initiative is as important in competition as it is in war. Gaining the initiative means our competitor must react to us. We can gain it by presenting a dilemma to our competitor, and also by setting the tempo of the activity taking place.

Marines must assume that potential competitors understand initiative as well as we do, thus they will take actions in order to gain the initiative. Many competitors also seek to create ambiguity about their actions, which leads to a problem of *attribution*. If we are not certain who performed an action, then we cannot attribute that action to any particular actor. This often delays our response and slows our tempo. Conversely, the gray box, *"Deployed Units Using DCO to 'Name and Shame'"* describes how if we improve understanding of our competitor, we can be primed to attribute their actions in ways that slow their tempo instead.

While competition essentially always exists, its intensity varies over the course of time. We must also understand that the long timelines involved in competition mean decisions and actions sometimes play out over months or years—even decades in some cases. This often results in opportunistic behavior, as rivals take advantage of conditions to achieve their strategic goals without

---

> ### Deployed Units Using DCO to 'Name and Shame'
>
> Defensive cyberspace operations (DCO) assist Marines in countering collections and attacks that take place in the cyber domain. Competitors of all kinds constantly try to penetrate the networks of deployed Marine units. Defensive cyberspace operations help keep those networks safe and functioning.
>
> Some DCO capabilities can help identify (or *attribute*) who is trying to penetrate these networks. Identifying who the bad actors are "names" them. Sharing this information publicly can "shame" them.
>
> Marine units can use DCO to name and shame by submitting a concept of operations up through the chain of command to the relevant combatant commander before they deploy. Once deployed and with an approved concept of operations, if the DCO capabilities are able to attribute network penetration attempts, then whoever made the attempt can be named and then shamed.
>
> This is an example of a cross-domain competitive act.

crossing the violence threshold (or crossing it briefly and then returning below the threshold before triggering war). Opportunity is often created when conditions change suddenly or temporarily, such as when a pandemic strikes. This diverts attention and resources, which creates a gap for an alert competitor to exploit.

Having no fixed timeline for achieving goals plus opportunism also leads to *incrementalism*, which is the effort to achieve a goal by adding together a number of small steps taken on the path toward it.

Achieving our goals in competition requires action, which comes from making decisions. Therefore what Marines are taught for warfighting serves them well here, provided they also apply judgment in recognizing how timelines can differ between war and the rest of the competition continuum.

CONCLUSION

Like war, competition serves policy, but usually does so over longer spans of time. These long timelines lead us to look for policy's aims in our enduring national interests, with aspects of these interests emphasized by the current state of domestic politics.

Attraction is an important concept in our theory of competition. It uses incentives and rewards to get another political actor to act in ways that are aligned with our interests. Attraction works directly, like when the United States provides economic or military aid (as in the example of the Philippines in the early 1950s). It also works indirectly through positive US narratives communicated through the informational element of national power.

Coercion is another important component of our theory. It takes two forms: compellence (to cause a rival to take action favorable to our goals) and deterrence (to cause a rival to not take an action). In war, we impose our will on an enemy. With coercion, we need our rival's cooperation because they must decide to comply with our wishes, even if their cooperation is unwilling.

The existence of the Marine Corps is a coercive tool for the Nation, if its competitive advantage is made clear to a rival.

Competitors act like systems; they have many parts that interact with each other in complex, often unpredictable ways. This also means competitors have strengths and weaknesses. As competition unfolds over time, the rival systems sense what their competitor is trying to do and adapt or evolve in an effort to improve their competitive advantage. They will often blend the threat of violence, or the use of violence itself, with other tools to gain an advantage. This constantly shifting mixture can get confusing, which is part of the goal. Competitors often intend for this confusion to help them reach their goals by causing their rivals to hesitate. This also helps them gain the initiative, so that they can set the pace for the competition.

Chapter 3

Preparing for Competition

The most important task for Marines and the Marine Corps is to recognize that we are always competing. Even choosing to do nothing is a competitive decision, it just happens to be one that surrenders the initiative to our competitors.

COMPETITION AND THE MARINE CORPS

Marines and the Marine Corps are tools for the Nation to use in the enduring competition that takes place in international relations. Every day, Marine capabilities and force posture affect the thinking of our competitors and potential adversaries. The more credible the Marine Corps, the more attractive we are to allies and partners. The more credible the Marine Corps is as a deterrent force, the more we affect our potential rivals' thinking.

The Banana Wars and Monroe Doctrine

Marines deployed frequently for the so-called Banana Wars in the Caribbean during the 1920s and 1930s. These were the "hybrid wars" of the times, with activities taking place on both sides of the violence threshold.

These deployments served vital US interests as well. The presence of the Marines was used as diplomatic and informational tools. Their presence was a way for the United States to signal to European powers to stay out of the Caribbean (and away from the Panama Canal) in accordance with the Monroe Doctrine.

For Marines, participation in our Nation's competitions starts at recruitment. The quality level of individuals brought into the Service provides the raw material to build a credible force. Attributes like education level, physical fitness, and mental resilience determine how quickly these individuals can be transformed into members of a coherent, capable organization. These attributes also help establish the range of possibilities available to adapt the existing force or innovate to create a new one.

Historically, the Marine Corps has been the Nations' hybrid force, conducting activities that straddled the line between violence and non-violence. Marines have often deployed to places to help the local people in time of need while being ready to restore order in those same places, if required.

The direction for the Marine Corps to be "most ready when the Nation is least ready" applies as much to competition as it does to war. In fact, this statement itself can be viewed as a competitive act in the informational element of national power.

Competing on NATO's Northern Flank

The Norway Air-Landed Marine Expeditionary Brigade Program was initiated in 1981 to reinforce NATO's northern flank. The goal of the program was to allow NATO forces in the region to be quickly reinforced, with equipment pre-positioned in Norway allowing a fast response. The higher level aim of the program was to deter Soviet aggressiveness.

Following the Cold War, the program was used to support worldwide Marine deployments. Equipment was modernized in recent years as part of a renewed focus on deterring Russian aggression.

CAMPAIGNING MINDSET

Competition is enduring in nature at the national level and the military element normally plays a supporting role, especially on the spectrum of competition short of war. This leads us to develop a campaigning mindset about competition, which is characterized by long-term thinking and recognition that we need to integrate our actions with others. Marines compete as part of a naval and joint force, but also as part of the interagency in an approach that combines all the elements of national power. Marines should strive to integrate our allies and partners into our competitions as this will increase our options while also increasing the potential number of dilemmas we can present to our rivals.

The cultivation of humility is also important for this mindset. Marines learn early on about the observe, orient, decide, act loop or OODA loop. Understanding of OODA teaches us that each *decision* is a hypothesis that gets tested in the real world when we *act*. The campaigning mindset then includes the understanding that we base our plans on a model we created of our competitor. Our decisions about how to achieve our goals in the competition are theories. Our plans then need to have the feedback loops built into them to either confirm that our models and theories are correct enough to help us reach our goals, or that we need to modify them.

Competition campaigning introduces the idea of *persistence*; strategic competition is more like a marathon than a sprint. Competition's enduring nature means that any campaign will require long-term commitment to achieve its goals. We also need to be alert for how our competitive advantages (and those of our rivals) will shift over time.

PROFESSIONALISM

"As military professionals charged with the defense of the Nation, Marine leaders must be true experts in the conduct of war." This statement from MCDP 1 establishes the first priority for Marines, which is to defend the Nation. As professionals,

---

> **Writing Computer Code at the Tactical Edge**
>
> Computer chips and the software that provide them their operating instructions are everywhere throughout the joint force, embedded in equipment, sensors, and communication systems. In the Marine Corps, it is rare that Marines in deployed tactical units write, re-write, or update software in order to streamline operations or to stay ahead of an adaptive enemy— but this is beginning to change.
>
> Two Marines on a SPMAGTF-CR-CC deployment independently wrote software to give them a competitive advantage. One automated the sorting of signals intelligence, separating signals of interest from noise. Another created electronic triggers for IEDs, then developed procedures to defeat them so the team could stay a step ahead of an adaptive enemy.
>
> This kind of activity will soon become the norm instead of ad hoc exceptions. The software integrated into our warfighting equipment will need to be adapted in order to retain competitive advantage versus thinking rivals.

Marines recognize this defense as a vital and enduring national interest. Our professionalism is grounded in our Nation's values, which sets us apart from competitors.

Achieving that standard—being prepared to defend the Nation— has been and will continue to be a competitive act. We accept that the existence of the Marine Corps helps deter potential foes. Our goal is for that deterrence to take place below the violence threshold. Professionals understand this goal and thus direct their energies (self-study and unit development in particular) toward achieving it.

As professionals, we recognize that development of coercive tools must be balanced with the need to attract in competition as well. For example, one component of an attraction strategy could lead to greater deterrence through building increased interoperability with an ally. It could also lead to advances through the informational element of national power as we perform a disaster relief mission. Marines must remain alert for the opportunities to use and integrate both coercion and attraction into the larger competition.

MCDP 1 also instructs that the "military profession is a thinking profession." This means that Marines must practice the mental discipline necessary to challenge our assumptions. As professionals, we need to dispassionately assess the environment and make certain we are setting the pace for our competitors.

EDUCATION

Professional military education for Marines intends to develop creative, thinking leaders in a continuous, progressive process of development. This philosophy aligns well with the kind of education Marines need to succeed in competition as well as in war. While the nature of competition endures over extended periods, like war its character constantly evolves. Rivals continually strive to improve their competitive advantages, strive to gain the initiative, and strive to keep their competitors off balance.

> ### Competitive Lessons From *The Innovator's Dilemma*
>
> This book examines how well-managed companies lose market dominance, even if they "have their competitive antennae up, listen astutely to their customers, and invest aggressively in new technologies."
>
> Successful and well-established companies excel at *sustaining* innovations, which create incremental improvements to their existing competitive advantages. Over time, they attract the type of people and develop procedures that are very good at making existing methods and technology better. However, these companies become quite vulnerable to *disruptive* innovation, because the people in the organization struggle to understand how the disruptive methods and technology can create competitive advantage.
>
> Eastman Kodak is a classic example. The company invented digital photography, but could not figure out how to create a market from it. Others were able to create a market-winning strategy from this disruptive technology, and they ultimately displaced Eastman Kodak from the top of its industry.

Education is a primary method for Marines to sustain competitive advantage over time. As Marine leaders progress through their careers, they need to develop mastery of the concepts that provide an ability to lead organizations like the Marine Corps through the cycles of innovation that are essential to staying at the forefront of competition. These concepts go beyond just adaptation. They include topics like organizational learning, the ability for an organization to sense changes in its environment and improve its effectiveness and efficiency in response to those changes; change management, when leaders are able to implement needed change in an organization while keeping its people engaged; and the difference between sustaining and disruptive innovation, which is essentially the difference between incremental improvements of what already exists versus new and better approaches that displace the old methods over time.

It is not enough for Marines to educate themselves on war and warfighting alone. Such a narrow focus limits the benefit they can give to the Nation. Most of a Marine's career will be spent training in the FMF or serving in the supporting establishment. Understanding competition and how the Marine Corps contributes to it is an essential skill, especially for career Marines who will have the greatest impact on the Marine Corps' competitive attributes over time. Self-education in social, economic, technological, and other matters beyond military history and leadership are essential if Marines are to excel in competition.

The goal for education then is to foster awareness, within the campaigning mindset, of how all the capabilities available to Marines can fit into and support a larger competition strategy. It should improve knowledge of and openness to the interests of potential and existing allies and partners. The outcome we seek from education is to increase the ability of Marines to envision greater possibilities in competition.

TALENT MANAGEMENT

Our doctrine of maneuver warfare places a premium on individual judgment and action, which also means we recognize all Marines of a given grade and occupational specialty are not interchangeable. They should be assigned to billets based on specific ability and temperament. This expression of talent management found in *Warfighting* applies equally as well to competing.

People have different strengths and weaknesses. The organizations that compete most effectively place their people in position to use their strengths. They also coach their people on development of their strengths, and link their use to the organization's goals. Some people excel at planning and creating new designs for operations and organizations. Others excel at taking a blueprint and then optimizing it so it works as well as possible. Few have the ability to do all of these things with equal skill. To compete at peak effectiveness, Marine leaders need to measure the talents of the people they lead and then match these skills to the duties they perform. Organizations that do this well and for a sustained period also have a sustained competitive advantage—they maximize the performance of their people over time.

FORCE PLANNING

Force planning (which includes the functions of design, development, and management of the force) for the Marine Corps must balance utility at many points on the competition continuum with building a force that is a functional tool for the joint force to use in winning battles. The output of this complex undertaking must serve the needs of competing generally and of warfighting in particular. Realizing that they both exist on the same continuum and that they are interrelated shapes our overall approach to this planning. This places a premium on the preceding discussion, as things like education and a campaigning mindset shape our ability to generate options for use in force planning.

To do this successfully, the output of our force planning should present a dilemma to our potential competitors and defeat their plans against us. The way we combine our organization, doctrine, training, and equipment should produce a competitive advantage (or multiple advantages). The options we choose within each of these elements affects our competitiveness over time. For example, if we enhance the training for equipment mechanics so that they can operate for extended periods without external support, then we also enhance our ability to operate in austere environments for long periods of time. The output of force planning is the sum of the choices made inside each of these elements. These choices must be guided by the goal of establishing competitive advantages, which are useful for combat and are also useful for competition.

If we are to fully prepare, then Marines need to also consider the merits and challenges of asymmetry in competition. Truly asymmetric competitive actions can impose costs on a rival. For example, the original "Assault Breaker" concept developed in the 1970s and 1980s was an asymmetric response to the Soviet advantage in armor and numbers. "Assault Breaker" linked

---

Staying Competitive in an Era of Tactical Nukes

In the second half of the 1950s, the Marine Corps organized itself for innovation. The problem Marine leaders faced was how to stay competitive in an era when tactical nuclear weapons could be used with devastating effect against the massing of ships required for the amphibious operations of that period.

Marine Corps Test Unit No. 1 was created to experiment and validate new tactics and techniques related to operating under threat of tactical nuclear weapons. The Hogaboom Board (named for board president LtGen Robert E. Hogaboom) developed helicopterborne methods for the assault waves of amphibious operations, so that shipping and shore-based elements could disperse and mitigate the effects of nuclear weapons.

This work had lasting impact on the organization and equipping of the FMF in 1950s and early 1960s. More importantly from a competition standpoint, it made the Marine Corps a credible deterrent force despite the threat of tactical nuclear weapons.

together improved sensors with precision munitions to negate the Soviet advantages. Today, China often projects power asymmetrically through coordinated use of all three of its Armed Forces' sea components: the People's Liberation Army Navy, Coast Guard, and Maritime Militia. China regularly employs the latter two sea forces on the front lines of East and South China Sea disputes and related incidents. The many historical examples of asymmetry in competition reinforces the value of the campaigning mindset, and of education. Actively seeking and then employing asymmetric advantages can place us in a beneficial position relative to our competitors; Marines need to stay alert for when they try to do the same to us.

The execution of force planning starts a cycle that begins with putting forth a theory about how we can contribute to the Nation's strategic competitions throughout the continuum, building the capabilities to bring the theory to reality, and then testing the capabilities through exercises and operations. Other political actors observe this theory unfold and adapt themselves so they can compete more effectively against it. Our observation of these adaptations starts the cycle once again.

Force planning then is a continual effort to stay ahead of potential adversaries. Thus we see that force planning itself is a competitive act, and the Marine Corps must retain the ability to reconfigure the force when necessary to sustain its competitive advantage, or to develop new ones. This ability starts with the mental flexibility that comes from humility and the disciplined practice of questioning assumptions.

Our awareness of the competition continuum and its existence both above and below the threshold of violence broadens our view on force planning. Our philosophy is that we can, as we have done in the past, prepare Marines to succeed in competition without sacrificing the Marine Corps' ability to prevail in battle. Our understanding of ourselves must include how the Marine Corps fits into the complex adaptive system that is the naval service and the joint force. We know that the Marine Corps has operated on both sides of the violence threshold and expect this to continue into the future. However, our campaigning mindset should lead us to explore thoroughly how the Marine Corps can contribute to preventing war by regularly operating below the violence threshold, even as Marines are ready to operate above it when required.

CONCLUSION

The Marine Corps is one of the Nation's tools for the strategic competition that is the normal state of events in international relations. As professionals, Marines acknowledge this condition and prepare themselves and the Marine Corps to succeed in this struggle. Adopting a campaigning mindset helps us do this effectively, as it aids us in visualizing the long timelines that often span years and decades. This influences the type of education they seek, to prepare them for the continual innovation that will be required to sustain competitive advantage and create new ones over the course of a long-term campaign. It also influences their thinking on talent management, because the most competitive organizations are the ones that get the most from their people by placing them in positions to use their strengths on a regular basis. All of this preparation leads to the type of agile force planning needed in long-term competition, resulting in a succession of force planning outcomes that achieve and then sustain competitive advantages in the military element of national power.

Chapter 4

How Rivals Approach Competition

A friend of mine says that to try to describe what life is like in Russia to someone who has never been there is like trying to describe the mysteries of love to a person who has never experienced it.[19]

—George Kennan

[C]ompeting effectively requires knowing your competition intimately. Only by understanding a competitor's worldview, decision making, and behavioral proclivities can one outmaneuver that competitor; only by grasping a rival's weaknesses and fears can one exploit them. Such understanding, in turn, requires sustained intellectual and economic investment.[20]

—Hal Brands

THE TEST

This chapter explores how political actors who view themselves as rivals to the United States and its allies approach competition.

Usually this means states with authoritarian governments or non-state actors who ascribe to an extremist ideology. We label these actors "rivals" because they either use competitive methods that run counter to accepted international norms or they pursue interests that clash with those of the United States and its allies; frequently they do both.

Truly understanding how our potential rivals approach competition requires serious reflection and critical thinking. Without such intellectual discipline, it will be nearly impossible for Marines to see beyond their own patterns of thought, the patterns they developed from living in American society and serving in an organization like the Marine Corps. However, those who do this kind of intellectual work give themselves the opportunity (as discussed in chapter 2) to create a model representing rival approaches to competition.

We return to the OODA loop to develop our understanding of why others approach competition differently and what the implications might be. We accept that OODA is more than a linear process; a person's *orientation* interacts dynamically with the other three elements of the OODA loop. Below we examine how a rival's *orientation* may be different from ours and then look at how to use this knowledge to build our understanding of rival approaches to competition.

Differing Orientations

Orientation's Effect on the OODA Loop

Orientation influences all other elements of the OODA loop, because it controls how people make sense of what they *observe* and because it shapes their *decisions* and *actions. Orientation* consists of all the things that affect how a person understands the world, such as language, culture, genetics, education, previous experience, etc. Humans often use mental shortcuts (called heuristics) they developed from their *orientation*. For example, when people learn to drive a car they gain experience in making a right turn. At first, they consciously think through each step, such as engaging the turn signal, looking in their mirrors for other traffic, tapping the brake pedal, turning the wheel, etc. In a relatively short time this experience becomes a mental shortcut so that when a driver recognizes a pattern their brain knows as "right turn," they automatically go through the steps of making the turn with little or no need to apply conscious thought to it. A similar type of mental shortcut also happens with great frequency, often in far more complex or dangerous situations.

It is essential for Marines to understand the role a person's *orientation* plays in the choices they make and how this relates to the actions they take in the world. This also applies to groups of people, where a kind of collective *orientation* can work in a similar way. We must consciously study the components of a rival's *orientation* if our understanding of their approach to competition is to be useful crafting our own campaign. Keep in mind that two people can look at a set of facts and come to very different conclusions about what these facts mean; this applies to groups of people as well. As we learned in chapter 2, narratives are what people use to give meaning to facts. A narrative in this sense is the story that explains how the world works. This narrative, or story, is constructed from the components (language, culture, experience, etc.) found in *orientation*. Thus, people make sense of the world based on their *orientation*.

Language Shapes Behavior

People use words to describe the things around them and to describe what is happening in the world. These words influence their actions. Language affects groups of people in a similar way, as the words they choose provide the meaning they want to communicate to each other. The meaning that is understood then causes the group to act in one way or another. Note that this applies to the word "competition." In the Western world, the word has various meanings that bring to mind sporting events or perhaps two businesses trying to win market share. When we add descriptors to the word, like "great power" competition or "nation-state" competition, the context the descriptors provide adjusts our understanding of the kind of "competition" we face.

Compare the Western use of "competition" to the words authoritarian governments use to label the same relationship; the contrast helps us see how language might shape behavior. For example, some rivals use "struggle" or "embracing while fighting" to name what we know as "competition."[21] To most Marines, hearing something described as "struggle" or "fighting" would shape an initial reaction quite a bit different than if we heard it described as "competition," because of the mental shortcuts built into how we learned to use the words and what our experience tells us those words typically mean. This should alert us that we need to employ critical thinking when considering the language our competitors use. It can (and does) cause them to approach the situation from a different perspective, which leads them to consider using different tools than we might choose.

The words people pick to describe things can also reveal biases or tendencies, and these can be exploited. Our competitors across the globe recognize Western societies' tendency to think of themselves as in either a condition of "at peace" or "at war." This is a significant contrast from Mao Zedong's "Politics is war without bloodshed, while war is politics with bloodshed." Mao chose the word "war" to describe the enduring relationship between political actors and in essence said that while the relationship is violent some of the time, it is always a state of war. Marines must consider how using words like these differs from how the United States describes it, and the corresponding impact these differences might have on the ways and means a rival might use in competition.

Culture

The culture of a group can be defined as the group's accumulated shared learning of how to solve internal and external problems. The group then determines that this shared learning is valid, so new members learn it as the correct way to perceive, think, feel, and behave. The group then starts to take this accumulated learning for granted, as a system of beliefs, values, and behavioral norms. When this happens, the system turns into basic assumptions and eventually drops out of conscious awareness.[22] Culture is analogous to a computer's operating system; it is the basic ruleset about how the computer works, but it operates in the background. We have to purposefully examine the operating system if we want to learn how it affects the computer's operations. Culture is like this ruleset, operating in the background while influencing a group's thoughts and actions. (Culture, like an operating system, receives updates and adjustments over time as more is learned and it adjusts to new threats and opportunities. Culture, however, changes organically while an operating system relies on human intervention.) Although culture has a wide variety of attributes, we will highlight time, risk, and mindset as we consider how culture might affect the way our rivals approach competition.

Collectivist or group-focused cultures emphasize the importance of the group over the individual and often feel compelled to reach decisions by gaining consensus, which frequently takes time to develop. From an American *orientation*, this may appear to take too long; from a collective culture *orientation*, achieving consensus might be considered so important that taking months or even years to reach a decision is given higher priority. Neither perspective is objectively "right" or "wrong," but each is logically consistent when viewed from its respective cultural *orientation*.

Different *orientations* also result in different attitudes toward identifying and weighing risk. This may lead to behavior that is surprising to us. For example, Chinese and Russian ships and aircraft have maneuvered in close proximity to US forces, which appears to us as unnecessarily dangerous and operating against agreed international protocols.[23] We may especially view such behavior as strange when we think of ourselves as "at peace" with them. Taking these risks might look quite different from another viewpoint; operating this way may seem justified to those who see themselves in a condition of "war without bloodshed" or "embracing without fighting."

Finally, different cultures produce different mindsets. As mentioned above, culture is a system of beliefs, values, and behavioral norms that operate in the background below the level of conscious awareness. This produces a frame of mind that seeks to make the "right" choice in a given situation, with "right" being defined by these background factors. This is also often labeled intuition. When someone makes an intuitive choice while within their own culture, the choice is often judged as a correct one by others from that culture. This is because the criteria they use to determine if it is correct aligns with the beliefs, values, and norms that originally informed the intuitive choice. However, people from a different culture have different judging criteria, originating from different values, beliefs, and norms, which leads them to intuitive choices likely quite different from ours. It will be difficult for people to explain why they made these choices because the criteria they used are below conscious thought.

How rivals view
THE COMPETITIVE ENVIRONMENT

Rivals operating from within different systems often perceive that they are under threat, especially competitors with authoritarian governments (the gray box on page 4-9 describes one example of these perceptions).[24] Regime survival is usually the top priority in these states.

These rivals look for opportunities to reduce the perceived threats while also working to expand their competitive options.

Our rivals constantly study the elements of US national power in an effort either to offset US advantages or to find seams to exploit. For example, the Soviet Union during the Cold War developed an elaborate system to measure the "correlation of forces" between the United States and USSR, which was further broken down into the correlation of economic forces, the correlation of military forces, etc.[25] This thought process heavily influences Russia today as they continue to deeply study the United States. Sun Tzu's famous statement to "know your enemy and know yourself" highlights a perhaps even deeper cultural imperative for China to study the United States and the West.

Finally, some rivals have a different outlook about the legitimacy of using aggressive action (like offensive cyber operations, interference in another state's internal politics, disinformation, etc.) to change the status quo in international relations. Their actions show they do not feel bound by standing international agreements and norms, unless they can use those agreements to

**Perceptions of Threat:
Russia's Attitude Toward NATO Evolves**

Many Russians hold the view that they tried to become partners with (and even considered joining) NATO during the 1990s, following the collapse of the Soviet Union. In their view, the relationship turned negative as they believed NATO (and the United States in particular) ignored their interests and failed to treat Russia as a great power.

Russians likely started to see NATO as a potential threat by 1999, as many of them were "appalled by NATO's bombing raids against Serbia," a country with close ties to Moscow. Several US policies in the 2000s created concern, including support to the color revolutions in Georgia and Ukraine, US plans for antiballistic missile defense, and the invasion of Iraq without a UN mandate.

Russia perceived increasing threats from the United States and NATO after 2007, believing they were "actively and intentionally threatening Russia." These perceived threats included openness to Georgia and Ukraine joining NATO, and support for the Arab Spring and military action against Libya. Vladimir Putin apparently drew a direct connection from the Arab Spring to threats against his regime.

This example highlights the power of *orientation* to affect people's decisions and actions. It is arguable whether the United States and the West intended to disrespect Russia's great power status, or use support for Arab democracy as a threat. However, Russian leaders perceived these actions a threat to their country and particularly their regime, which clearly affected their competitive choices. They now use this as a powerful narrative to justify their actions.

their advantage. Instead, their behavior shows they recognize resource constraints or hard power deterrence as the only kind of limits they might respect.

DIFFERING APPROACH TO COMPETITION CAMPAIGNING

All the above leads to a permanent struggle mindset. There is no "at peace" condition, even when they choose to cooperate in a particular area. It becomes a question of *when* and *how* they will compete, not *if* they will be competing. With this as the mindset, the tools used to create competitive advantages are limited only by human creativity and available resources. These rivals might take an action primarily to advance their economy, but they will also attempt to leverage that action to gain an advantage. This mindset causes them to try and exploit any chance they see emerging. When they believe their competitors are distracted by other world events, they will seize on any opportunity this presents.

The following are common characteristics[26] of our rivals' approach to competition:

- Strong central command and control.
- Clear strategic goals.
- Powerful narratives.
- Weaponization of benign activities.[27]

- Recruitment of ethnic diasporas.
- Domination of ethnic media.
- Interference in local politics.
- Strong enforcement action.
- Fostering relationships with local groups, including criminal and terrorist organizations.
- Assertion of extra-territorial rights.
- Intelligence and covert operations.
- Encouragement of dependencies.
- Powerful military cover.
- Expanded concept of combined arms.[28]
- Acceptance of high levels of risk.
- Postured for the long-term.

They combine these characteristics in novel and innovative ways to pursue their goals while taking advantage of United States and its allies' blind spots (like being "at peace").

A RIVAL CONCEPT FOR COMPETITION

The Idea of a "Theory of Victory" Applied to Competition

MCDP 1, *Warfighting,* explains how the Marine Corps uses maneuver warfare to shatter an enemy's cohesion through a variety of rapid, focused, and unexpected actions which create a turbulent and rapidly deteriorating situation with which the enemy cannot cope. This is maneuver warfare's theory of victory, to splinter the enemy's system so that it can no longer function effectively.

**Weaponization of Benign Activities:
Tourism in Targeted Countries**

Palau is an island nation strategically located east of the Philippines, has only 20,000 citizens, and maintains diplomatic relations with Taiwan. About 2014, China put Palau on its approved list for overseas tourism.

By 2015, Chinese tourists flooded Palau, created a Chinese-funded hotel construction boom, and bought up buildings and apartments. Chinese-owned restaurants and small businesses also started, displacing local enterprises. Chinese tour groups were typically self-contained, staying in Chinese-owned hotels and bringing their own tour guides, which froze out locally owned tourism businesses. The influx of Chinese tourism created divisions between Paulauans benefiting from the tourism and those threatened by the displaced businesses, increased living costs, and damage to the local environment brought by the tourism flood.

In late 2017, Beijing placed Palau off-limits for package tours, dramatically affecting Palau's economy. The off-limits order was reportedly an effort to put pressure on Taiwan via their relationship with Palau. China used tourism to create an economic dependency and then manipulated it to help them achieve their aims.

We can apply the idea of a theory of victory to competition to discern how rivals approach it. Each rival uses its own theory in competition, but we can make some useful generalizations Marines can use to analyze specific competitors. First, each of this class of rival governs itself through an authoritarian power structure with regime survival as the top priority. This heavily influences all the other competitive choices made, both domestically and internationally, in these rivals' theories.

Next, these rivals strive to avoid war with the United States and its allies. Note that war is not the same as violence. These rivals will selectively cross over the threshold of violence against the United States or its allies and partners, but will be careful to keep a tight rein on it so that it does not escalate into war (these discrete pulses of violence can be useful for boundary stretching and to create hesitation). *This is not a fixed principle; as rivals continue to study the United States, there may come a time when they believe baiting the United States or its allies into war gives them an advantage if they also believe they have developed the strength to prevail.*

With these two principles as background, our rivals approach competition as a constant state of being so every decision and action affects it. Thus, they are either setting conditions that will make it easier to achieve their goals, or they are reaching their goals through slow increments or opportunistic lunges.

We can summarize their theory of "victory in competition" like this: these rivals think of the relationship as "winning without fighting" or "winning war before it starts" and not as "competition"; regime survival is the number one goal, and they

> **Expanded Concept of Combined Arms:**
> **Iran's Many Competitive Tools**
>
> Iran uses an impressive array of tools to compete in the Middle East and beyond. It blends all elements of national power under its control into a new 21st century form of combined arms that works well in a framework prioritizing regime survival and avoiding war.
>
> Iran integrates many combined arms tools into its approach to competition. The wide variety includes everything from information and cyber operations, energy diplomacy, and covert operatives, to proxy forces in multiple countries throughout the region. It blends these together with other economic tools and the various arms of its military in a persistent, gradual approach to achieving its goals.
>
> These elements are combined through the direction of a central authority.

believe their regime is constantly under threat, so the competition is one of perpetual struggle; every action they take shapes the environment to make it easier to reach their goals, either domestically or internationally. In this environment, they are either incrementally moving toward their goals or on the alert to seize one if an opportunity presents itself.

The Concept Illustrated

We will use a hypothetical model to illustrate a concept for this approach to competition. First, the objectives will be set by a strong, centralized authority. Outside observers might not completely understand how consensus on these objectives was achieved (as discussed in chapter 1, there may be multiple centers of power in a rival), but once they are agreed upon they will usually endure until changed or updated by the central authority. These objectives will then be framed by a powerful narrative that is tailored to multiple audiences. Of particular note, each of these rivals will make certain the narrative serves to build and sustain support among its domestic audiences (see the "*A Hypothetical Scenario: The Baltics*" gray box on the next page).[29] With regime survival as the highest priority, the authorities will always seek to bolster internal support.

These rivals study their competitors continuously and deeply. They use this study to inform their own OODA loop. As they make decisions and take action, they take advantage of feedback loops to learn what worked and what didn't, so that they can refine their approach to become more effective.

They will constantly try to shape the environment so that when an opportunity to make progress toward a goal presents itself, conditions for a rapid advance are already established to the greatest extent possible. This condition setting is persistent, its enduring nature springs from the permanent struggle mindset. This lends itself to leveraging every action for multiple advantages. Tourism into a smaller country may seem benign, but it can also create an economic dependency. Once the smaller country starts to rely on the income the tourism generates, the authoritarian rival can threaten to cut it off unless their demands are met. Domination of ethnic media and recruiting ethnic diasporas illustrate other shaping activities. Using economic strength to squeeze out other ethnic media channels or to simply buy competing media outlets generates the ability to target messages at, and control the information to, diasporas. At a minimum, this creates sympathy for the rival, but it can also be used to manipulate the diaspora living in the targeted country.[30]

A Hypothetical Scenario: The Baltics

Observers have outlined a hypothetical Russian attempt to seize a part of a Baltic state, using "defense" of native Russian speakers living there as justification (25% of both Latvia and Lithuania's population are native Russian speakers).

In such a scenario, Russia could shape the action by transmitting their narrative on Russian language media broadcast into the Baltics to build sympathy and support among the Russian diaspora. Cyber and media operations could be used to slow a NATO response, to confuse decision making in the Baltic countries, and to spread disinformation around the globe. Nuclear posturing, especially ambiguity about what could trigger their use, would also cause hesitation. Russia could place smart mines and unmanned underwater vehicles in the Baltic Sea to limit NATO's maritime response options.

Russia could then send military units in unmarked uniforms or mercenary equivalents across the border, to join forces with sympathizers in the diaspora. Swarms of small but lethal drones, electronic warfare, and loitering smart munitions would cover these actions locally. Sophisticated integrated air defenses located in Russia would extend their coverage far out to sea.

Hypothetically, this kind of operation could achieve its objectives in a *fait accompli*, seizing territory before NATO and the international community could react to prevent it.

Goals will be reached either slowly through the accumulation of small steps, or suddenly when an alert rival spots an opportunity and seizes it. Both efforts will be obscured by disinformation and deception as much as possible in order to create confusion and hesitation, especially in the minds of their competitors' decision makers. Both aspects will likely be used in actual practice.

Our brief illustration highlights one outline of how rivals might approach competition. There are many other possibilities. We need to study each rival in detail to develop understanding of how it is competing now and how it could approach competition in the future.

CONCLUSION

To compete effectively, Marines need to focus on their potential competitors, especially those who see themselves as rivals to the United States and its allies. Truly understanding these potential rivals requires serious reflection and critical thinking.

The OODA loop offers a model to examine why and how rivals approach competition differently. The strength of *orientation* affects all aspects of the model. The elements contained in a person or group's *orientation* (like language, culture, experience, etc.) work in the background. It takes deep study to first identify these elements and then to learn how they affect the *decisions* and *actions* a rival takes.

Rivals with authoritarian leadership approach competition differently than the United States and its allies. Regime survival is the top priority for them and so they want to find ways to compete that do not risk triggering a war with the United States. To do that and still reach their goals, they closely study the United States and its allies in an effort to develop ways and means to side step our strengths while exploiting any gaps they identify. Because they are authoritarian and can direct the action from a central authority, they have a wide range of tools available for use. Their mindset of perpetual struggle means they are constantly shaping the environment to make it easier for them to reach their goals at some point in the future. It also means they constantly take incremental steps toward their goals while remaining alert for the chance to pounce on them if an opportunity arises.

Chapter 5

The Conduct of Competition

THE CHALLENGE

The challenge is to develop a concept of competition for Marines that stays in balance with our preparation for war, remains consistent with our understanding of the nature and theory of competition, and accounts for the realities of international strategic competition.

MANEUVER WARFARE'S INFLUENCE

Marines can use maneuver warfare principles to great effect in competition. We still seek to achieve our goals in a flexible and opportunistic way. We seek to achieve a relative tempo advantage so that we gain the initiative. Marines' in-depth understanding of the OODA loop is relevant everywhere on the competition continuum. Marines should not seek to re-invent maneuver warfare for competition but rather think through how it can be applied across the competition continuum (and not just to the continuum's subset that deals with war and the various forms of warfare).

ORIENTING ON THE COMPETITOR

Orienting on the competitor is fundamental to successful competition. We develop our understanding of the competitor's system and then exploit the weaknesses we find in it. We develop models of the rival's system and then use these models to share our understanding of it with others. We then develop ways to test our model in the real world. We observe our tests, then use the feedback from these observations to improve the model. Marines learn about the OODA loop early in their service, which helps them move through this cycle smoothly. The nearby gray box provides an example of how the Joint Special Operations Task Force oriented on a rival and then changed itself so that it could become more effective than its competitor.[31]

MCDP 1 teaches that we should try to "get inside" an adversary's thought processes and see them as they see themselves so that we can set them up for defeat. It is essential that we understand our adversary on their own terms. We should not assume that every adversary thinks as we do, competes as we do, or shares our values or objectives.

> **Joint Special Operations Task Force**
> **Orients on Competitor**
>
> During Operation Iraqi Freedom, Al Qaeda in Iraq (AQI) initially
> had network and speed advantages over the traditionally
> organized, stove-piped task force. Al Qaeda in Iraq started out
> as a much faster and more agile organization, which made
> them more effective.
>
> By orienting on their competitor, the task force developed a
> model of how AQI worked and was able to change themselves
> in order to become even more effective. They did this by
> exploiting information technology, but even more so by
> breaking down stove-pipes inside the task force, building
> useful relationships with other organizations, and by pushing
> authority to the edges of the task force. By orienting on their
> rival, the task force created the ability to move faster, and more
> effectively, than AQI.

Marines and the Marine Corps are strong tools for our Nation to
compel or deter our rivals. As discussed in chapter 2, we know
that the target of our compellence or deterrence must cooperate
(even if they are unwilling) if we are to be effective. Our
knowledge of the competitor's system will help us understand
their thinking enough to make good judgments on how we can
force this (possibly unwilling) cooperation.

Marines and the Marine Corps are also strong tools in a strategy
of attraction. We can demonstrate our national values through
efforts such as humanitarian assistance operations, providing
highly credible support to the informational element of national
power. Marines regularly play a large role in building and then

sustaining relationships with allies and partners. Strong networks such as these increase our competitive options and create challenges for our competitors.

SHAPING THE ACTION

Our competition goals are derived from our vital national interests, and we must think ahead if Marines are to support reaching these goals. In thinking ahead we establish what we want to accomplish, why, and how. This provides a vision for succeeding in competition, which in turn helps align the actions taken toward reaching the goals.

In both the near- and long-term, we orient on our competitor to develop our understanding of their system. We continually refine our models of their system so that we can focus on their weaknesses, including increasing our understanding of how their culture affects their decision-making process. Similarly, we must try to see ourselves through our competitor's eyes in order to identify our own vulnerabilities that they may try to exploit. To influence the future, we consider how we can exploit our competitor's weaknesses while protecting our own. This usually takes the form of planning.

Our plans will not always produce a detailed timetable of events, as we accept that competitions may unfold over a long time. Instead, we attempt to shape the general conditions of the

> **Preventing Nazi Penetration
> of South America Before WW II**
>
> The US Government became concerned when Nazi Germany used Axis-owned airlines to establish footholds in South America in the late 1930s. Prior to United States' entry into the war, South American countries were reluctant to station US troops or equipment on their soil.
>
> To displace the Nazi airlines, the United States developed the Airport Development Program. Through this program, Pan American Airlines secretly acquired access to foreign airfields in Central and South America and the Caribbean and improved existing facilities on behalf of the US Government, without disclosing the government's role. The Axis-controlled airlines were replaced by Pan-American or local airlines by 1940.
>
> Following United States' entry into the war, these locations provided springboards in support of force projection into Africa and convoys to Britain.

competition. Since Marines support our larger national competitive effort, we first need to determine who we are supporting. This support, limited only by our imaginations and available resources, can take a variety of forms across all of our operating domains.

For example, our force posture exists in all domains and can contribute to deterrence in these domains. Through the diplomatic and informational elements of power, it can also improve relationships with our allies and partners. Force posture can help develop ties with partner militaries that lead to attracting top performing international officers to our Service schools, which further deepens the relationship. Expanding relationships like this shapes our campaign of competition by increasing the potential number of competitive actions we can take.

COMBINED ARMS

Combined arms is the full integration of arms in such a way that to counteract one, the enemy must become more vulnerable to another. We pose the enemy not just with a problem, but with a dilemma—a no-win situation. This is the way Marines fight and win battles. This idea also governs how Marines compete, even though we broaden "no-win" situations to include careful consideration of positive-sum options. The governing idea is to orchestrate all of our tools together in ways that are most favorable to us.

A combined arms mindset leads one to consider how to use the multi-domain tools of all potential partners in an effort to reach one's goals. The idea is to use all available resources to best advantage. Internal to the Marine Corps, we look to combine the complementary characteristics of different types of units to create a competitive advantage (like when we combine assault support aircraft with infantry so that we can concentrate more quickly than our adversary). Externally, we look to combine our capabilities with those of the joint force to create advantage. We apply the same mindset in competition when we combine our capabilities with those of our joint and interagency partners. For

---

Deception and Decoys

The ability to employ deception and decoys can provide a competitive advantage, even below the threshold of violence. Marines should add them both to their combined arms toolkit, in every domain.

Part of the rationale for distributed operations is to operate in a way that makes it harder to be targeted. For example, a platoon in marching formation is easier to target than a platoon that is operating as independent squads.

Deception and decoys act as multipliers to this distributed effect. Deception can mask unit locations. Decoys can make an adversary think they are looking at elements of a Marine unit, but what they really "see" is a false signature of that unit. Effective deception and decoys are *cost-imposing*, because the adversary has to expend greater resources to determine the verified location of the unit.

Deception and decoys can be cost-imposing below the threshold of violence. Many potential adversaries collect against our exercises, particularly those conducted with allies and partners. Effective deception and decoys employed in these exercises can cause doubt in the mind of these adversaries, which can lead them to spend resources on counters, resources that could have been used for something else.

example, a squad of infantry Marines combined with a single Coast Guardsman becomes a potent law enforcement element—the Coast Guard provides the law enforcement authorities while the Marines provide the manpower to search a vessel for contraband. This same mindset applies to combining the complementary characteristics of Marines with other partners,

---

**Share the Operating Picture,
Align Interests, Present a Dilemma**

In some parts of the world, the United States is at a disadvantage when it comes to numbers. Some competitors have local superiority in the numbers of people, ships, planes, etc. In many cases, local allies and partners of the United States are few in number as well, so they face the same disadvantage.

One way to overcome this is to combine the picture of the US sensor network with that of allies and partners. Sharing the same picture of a competitor will help align defense interests. It can also present the competitor a dilemma, as they are no longer able to isolate one outnumbered competitor.

This combined picture can be built in two ways. First, Marines can work toward this shared picture when conducting bi-lateral exercises. Second, Marines can help build this more permanently by working with the joint force and relevant combatant commands.

Modern technology is bringing this vision within reach. Previously, national classifications made this a challenge because the data could reveal sources and methods, which made it difficult to share the information. Now, application programming interfaces, or APIs, offer the chance for multiple users to be customers of the sensor data without knowing where it came from. It is becoming possible to share a common operating picture while still protecting sources and methods—and presenting our common competitor a dilemma at the same time.

whether they are from another US Government department or from an allied country. We orient on the competitor because we want to make sure the combined arms dilemma we intend to present in competition is actually a problem for them.

This mindset leads Marines to develop holistic plans designed to reach specific goals, in both war and along the larger competition continuum. In competition, the idea of "combined arms" extends through the joint force, interagency, to allies and partners. In planning, we should identify the capabilities each element could bring to the competition. Or, we could develop a plan and then identify our capability shortfalls, and then look outward for a partner to fill that gap. In either case, we would then determine how to obtain the necessary authorities so that these capabilities could be included in our combined arms approach to competition.

CAMPAIGN OF COMPETITION

Embracing the competition mindset leads to the realization that the Marine Corps plays an important but supporting role in our Nation's various competitions. This forms our approach to developing our campaigns of competition. Campaign goals are established by analyzing enduring interests and how they are being affected by current policy. For Marines, these goals are further refined by aligning them with the theater combatant commander's objectives at every point on the competition continuum, both in day-to-day operations below the violence threshold and in the event of contingencies (ideally, the theater objectives will be aligned with interagency goals as well).

By orienting on the competitor, we start to develop theories on how we can reach our campaign goals even though we are in competition with our rival. Like in a judo contest, in competition we must always be aware of our position relative to our opponent. We must seek a position of advantage and work constantly to either sustain it or to create a new one. If our goals are zero-sum relative to our rival, than we develop plans to either compel them to act in certain ways or deter them from taking action unfavorable to us. If our goals are positive-sum, then we can explore the use of additional ways to reach our goals. In reality, the ways and means we use to reach our goals are likely to be a mix of zero-sum and positive-sum.

Marines' understanding of the OODA loop leads us to conclude that the campaign choices we make in planning are hypotheses. The campaign actions we take test these hypotheses, and OODA's many feedback loops help us to refine our decisions/hypotheses to make them more effective and get us closer to our goals. In other words, if we take a certain action we anticipate our competitor will react in a certain way. Our observation of this reaction helps us understand whether our theory about how to reach our campaign goals was essentially correct, or if we need to adjust it so that we become more effective. The disciplined yet creative application of this process is what allows us to gain the initiative in competition and set its tempo.

Timelines associated with competition campaigns are often quite long, some extend over several decades. When considering competition campaign goals in light of these long timelines, it is often the case that it is better to take small steps toward the goal than it is to take large risks in an effort to achieve the goal in one swift move. The iterative nature of competition matched to the disciplined use of the OODA loop will help planners determine how aggressive one should be in pursuit of campaign goals. As a practical matter, this will ebb and flow over time. Changing conditions also lead to changes in how aggressive we can be.

Acknowledging these long timelines leads us to consider the consistency of our competitive goals. If we believe we may need to take many small steps toward a goal over the course of months, years, or decades, then our objectives should remain relatively stable during that time. This is why we look first to our national interests before we derive our competition campaigning goals; once those are determined we then decide how Marines can support achieving them. The gray box in chapter 2 discussing freedom of navigation offers a good example; this US interest has remained stable for centuries. How it has been achieved (and even the degree to which it has been achieved) has evolved continuously from the 1700s to today.

The campaigning mindset needs to be applied when considering competitive activities, especially long-term thinking and integrating our actions with others. Before beginning an activity, Marines should consider if we can sustain that activity long enough to move us toward our goal. We especially want to avoid imposing costs on ourselves that consume our resources at a rate we cannot support. Marines must also consider how our planned activities support and interact with those of our partners (naval and joint force, interagency, partner nations, etc.). Thus we need to consider up front what our partners are planning so that we can ensure our activities are complementary.

Consistency and sustainability lead us to consider the pace, or tempo, of competition. This tempo is often driven by a cycle of action and counteraction. When one rival commits a competitive act, others will respond and often try to counter it. This cycle could unfold over decades, like when NATO incrementally adds member nations to the organization. Or, action/counteraction could take seconds to complete in cyberspace. Marines need to understand the temporal aspects of competitive campaigns and how it is often tied to the cycle of action/counteraction.

Each campaign has a narrative, which provides context and purpose for the competition. Our narrative competes with that of our rival. To defeat a competitor's narrative we need to replace it with a more persuasive one. Simply denying someone's story may actually reinforce it in the minds of the target audience. That is why we need to replace it with a more compelling story. For example, two firms may sell an identical commodity. Their respective narratives will explain why they are the right choice to win the business of a particular customer. The stronger narrative will displace the weaker one.

Conclusion

Our warfighting philosophy of maneuver warfare is the philosophy that animates our approach to competition as well. Marines take the same flexible and opportunistic approach to competition as they do toward fighting battles.

The most important tenet of maneuver warfare is to orient on the enemy and this influence is also felt in competition; we orient on our competitor. We need to develop an understanding of our rival if we are to create an effective plan that will help us prevail in competition. We must understand their system, where it is strong, and where it is weak. This allows us to shape the environment by developing a clear vision for our competitive activities. This vision also allows us to identify the partners with whom we need to coordinate.

Marines fight using combined arms and we must compete in the same way. This is the foundational mindset for determining how we can present a dilemma to our competitor.

Marines and the Marine Corps are essential tools in our Nation's effort to advance our vital national interests. The Marine Corps makes its greatest contributions near the threshold of violence on the competition continuum. This means that individual Marines need to prepare themselves to act on both sides of the threshold, and to do so in disciplined ways that advance the Nation's interests.

Competing is a way of thinking. Like maneuver warfare, it is a state of mind born of boldness, intellect, initiative, and opportunism. It is about understanding our competitor's system so that we can develop, sustain, and adapt our competitive advantage, so that the Marine Corps will always be a useful tool for the Nation in the enduring competition that is the normal state of international relations.

Notes

1. MCDP-1 *Warfighting*, p. 4.

2. The Joint Staff, Joint Doctrine Note 1–19, *Competition Continuum*, 3 June 2019.

3. Encyclopedia Britannica, *Marshall Plan*, https://www.britannica.com/event/Marshall-Plan, accessed 2 June 2020.

4. Derived from: Gen David G. Perkins, USA, "Multi-Domain Battle: The Advent of Twenty-First Century War," *Military Review*, https://www.armyupress.army.mil/Portals/7/military-review/Archives/English/Multi-Domain-Battle-The-Advent-of-Twenty-First-Century-War.pdf?ver=2017-10-26-160929-763, accessed 2 June 2020.

5. "George F. Kennan, 'The Inauguration of Organized Political Warfare' [Redacted Version]," April 30, 1948, History and Public Policy Program Digital Archive, Obtained and contributed by A. Ross Johnson. Cited in his book 'Radio Free Europe and Radio Liberty', Ch1 n4. NARA release courtesy of Douglas Selvage. Redacted final draft of a memorandum dated May 4, 1948, and published with additional redactions as document 269, 'FRUS, Emergence of the Intelligence Establishment. 'https://digitalarchive.wilsoncenter.org/document/114320

6. MCDP 1 *Warfighting* p. 3-5.

7. National Commission on Terrorist Attacks upon the United States, *The 9/11 Commission Report: Final Report of the National Commission on Terrorist Attacks Upon the United States*, New York: Norton, 2004, xvi.

8. Ben Connable, Jason H. Campbell, and Dan Madden, "Stretching and Exploiting Thresholds for High-Order War: How Russia, China, and Iran Are Eroding American Influence Using Time-Tested Measures Short of War," RAND Corporation, 2016, p. ix.

9. Ibid, p. 17-20.

10. The Joint Staff, *Joint Concept for Integrated Campaigning*, 16 March 2018.

11. See "National Security Council Report, NSC 68, 'United States Objectives and Programs for National Security'," April 14, 1950, History and Public Policy Program Digital Archive, US National Archives. http://digitalarchive.wilsoncenter.org/document/116191, p. 5, and "United States Strategic Approach to The People's Republic of China," The White House, 2020, accessed 4 June 2020, https://www.whitehouse.gov/wp-content/uploads/2020/05/U.S.-Strategic-Approach-to-The-Peoples-Republic-of-China-Report-5.20.20.pdf, p. 1.

12. The gray box titled "Operation Outside the Box Demonstrates a Competitive Advantage" is derived from "Israel Shows Electronic Prowess," David A. Fulghum and Robert Wall, Aviation Week & Space Technology, 26 November 2007, http://aviationweek.com/awin/israel-shows-electronic-prowess.

13. Jerrold D. Green, Frederic Wehrey, and Charles Wolf, Jr., "Understanding Iran," RAND Corporation, 2009, pp. ix–xvi.

14. *Arms and Influence*, Thomas Schelling, Yale University Press, New Haven, CT, 1966, pp. 1–34.

15. "Coercion Theory: A Basic Introduction for Practitioners," Tami Davis Biddle, Texas National Security Review, accessed 14 May 2020, https://tnsr.org/2020/02/coercion-theory-a-basic-introduction-for-practitioners/.

16. "Deterrence and Coercive Diplomacy: The Contributions of Alexander George," Jack S. Levy, *Political Psychology*, Vol. 29, No. 4, 2008.

17. "Examining Complex Forms of Conflict: Gray Zone and Hybrid Challenges," Frank G. Hoffman, *Prism*, Vol. 7, No. 4, 2018, p. 36.

18. Ibid., p. 37-38. The definition was modified slightly by omitting "catastrophic" before terrorism and "in the battlespace" following criminal behavior. Hybrid warfare can feature all kinds of terrorism, not just catastrophic. Also, in today's connected world, all of the elements of hybrid warfare can be (and are) projected globally and are not necessarily confined to a specific battlespace, yet they can all be conducted in pursuit of desired political objectives they share in common.

19. George F. Kennan, "Planning of Foreign Policy," *Measures Short of War: The George F. Kennan Lectures at the National War College 1946–47*, Ed Giles D. Harlow and George C. Maerz, NDU Press, 1991, p. 207.

20. Hal Brands, "The Lost Art of Long-Term Competition," *The Washington Quarterly* • 41:4 pp. 31–51 https://doi.org/10.1080/0163660X.2018.1556559.

21. Ross Babbage, 'Ten questionable assumptions about future war in the Indo-Pacific', Australian Journal of Defence and Strategic Studies 2, 1 (2020): 27–45, http://www.defence.gov.au/ADC/publications/AJDSS/volume2-issue1/ten-questionable-assumptions-about-future-war-in-the-indo-pacific-babbage.asp.

22. Edgar H. Schein, *Organizational Culture and Leadership*, 5th ed., Wileym 2017, Kindle Edition, p. 6.

23. Ross Babbage, "Winning Without Fighting: Chinese and Russian Political Warfare Campaigns and How the West Can Prevail Volume I," Center for Strategic and Budgetary Assessments, 2019, p. 33.

24. Andrew Radin, Clint Reach, "Russian Views of the International Order," RAND, Santa Monica, CA, 2017, p. 1-30.

25. Michael J. Deane, "The Soviet Concept of the 'Correlation of Forces'," Stanford Research Institute, Arlington, VA, 1976, p. 3-5.

26. Ibid., p. 27-34.

27. Ross Babbage, "Winning Without Fighting: Chinese and Russian Political Warfare Campaigns and How the West Can Prevail Volume II: Case Studies," Center for Strategic and Budgetary Assessments, 2019, p. 23-25.

28. Michael J. Mazarr, "Mastering the Gray Zone: Understanding a Changing Era of Conflict," Strategic Studies Institute and United States Army War College Press, Dec 2015, p. 43-51.

29. "When China Fought America," *The Economist*, 3 Oct 2020.

30. Michael E. O'Hanlon, *The Senkaku Paradox: Risking Great Power War Over Limited Stakes*, Brookings Institution Press, Washington, D.C., 2019, (Kindle edition), p. 62-68.

31. *Team of Teams: New Rules of Engagement for a Complex World*, Stanley McChrystal, Tantum Collins, David Silverman, and Chris Fussell, Penguin Publishing Group, NY, 2015.

A non-cost copy of this document is available at:

https://www.marines.mil/News/Publications/MCPEL/

Copyright Information

This document is a work of the United States Government and the text is in the public domain in the United States. Subject to the following stipulation, it may be distributed and copied:

- Copyrights to graphics and rights to trademarks/Service marks included in this document are reserved by original copyright or trademark/Service mark holders or their assignees, and are used here under a license to the Government and/or other permission.
- The use or appearance of United States Marine Corps publications on a non-Federal Government website does not imply or constitute Marine Corps endorsement of the distribution service.

Printed in Poland
by Amazon Fulfillment
Poland Sp. z o.o., Wrocław
06 April 2023

592403ba-e73b-418f-bec2-ff5af4e13788R01